Dhan Gopal Mukherji (1890-1936) grew up in Bengal, before he moved to Japan and then the United States. In the US he started his writing career and went on to win much acclaim for his books. He wrote a number of books for children, including the prestigious Newbery Medal-winning *Gay-Neck, the Story of a Pigeon* (1927). His children's books include *Kari the Elephant*, *Hari the Jungle Lad*, *Ghond the Hunter*, *Hindu Fables*, *Fierce Face*, among others.

Also by the author in Talking Cub:

The Adventures of Sirdar

The Cat Who Became King

Praise for *The Adventures of Sirdar:*

'It allows kids...to embark on a roller coaster ride through the wild.'

—*Mint Lounge*

'If wild life fascinates you, then you will love reading this book.'

—*Telegraph, My Kolkata*

Fierce-Face the Tiger

Jungle Stories

DHAN GOPAL MUKHERJI

talking CUB
An Imprint of Speaking Tiger Books

SPEAKING TIGER PUBLISHING PVT. LTD
125A, Ground Floor, Shahpur Jat,
Near Asiad Village, New Delhi 110049

This edition published in paperback by Talking Cub in
Speaking Tiger Books 2023

ISBN: 978-93-5447-559-797
eISBN: 978-93-5447-548-1

10 9 8 7 6 5 4 3 2 1

Typeset in Adobe Garamond Pro by Jojy Philip
Printed at HT Media Ltd, Greater Noida

Contents

KARI
The Elephant

FIERCE-FACE

The Tiger

introduction

If the present story, the biography of a tiger, is scrutinized carefully, the discerning adult reader will notice a unique presentation of reality. It is a truism that the modern boys and girls do not see nor hear the way their grandparents did. The camera, the talking pictures and the radio have made changes that are perceptible. Eyes flit from object to object; ears hear more than one noise at a time; and the mind decides upon ideas with unprecedented speed.

In *Fierce-Face* I have sought to present some information about the jungle through the life of a tiger. But he moves and lives with a quickness and angularity that would satisfy the camera-bred eyes of our age. Those who read aloud to children will be able to read this story without being misunderstood. Certain simple reiterations and pauses have been placed so as to enable the listening youngsters to feel as if a voice from India is broadcasting.

I have not sacrificed my mystical beliefs. They are part and parcel of my inner being. But it behooves the artist in all of us to attempt to reach the young through their modes of sight, hearings, feeling and thinking. If the reader has the patience to read the following pages he will find in them the enchantment of the Indian jungle and the Hindu belief that Man, Nature, and animal life are but facets of the Divine.

D. G. M.

1

fierce-face

During the first two months of his life, Fierce-Face knew nothing of his father. His mother, Bagni, took good care to nurse him in secret.

Generally, fathers of the cat tribe detest their sons. They try to kill them. It is the great care that the mother takes in protecting her cubs that saves them from slaughter.

Until his skin had grown tough—tough enough to withstand another cat's slashing claw—Bagni did not present her child to his father.

Hardly had the second month passed when her husband located her. It was utterly unexpected. But nothing harmful took place. The cub and its sire seemed to make friends with each other instantly. Though this brought peace to the mother's heart, she did not relax her vigilance. After the thrill of their meeting had passed, Bagni took good care to remain between the two males while they marched from place to place. During the day, when her husband and son slept, she kept wide awake lying between them.

The cub's growth seemed to increase his mother's fondness for him. This the father resented. Each day he grew more and more irritable.

One night while the entire family was pursuing a Sambur deer, the cub got in the way, letting the prey escape. Angered beyond control, the elder cat fell upon him. The mother hurried to the scene. At a glance she realized the fatal strife. Her first impulse was to separate the two fighters. At that very moment a sudden howl of pain from Fierce-Face made her insane with anger. Like a cobra, she buried her teeth in the father's neck. As the male struck her with his claws, it dawned on her that on her safety depended that of her baby's. Her fears gave way to the loving fury of her motherhood. Her jaws gripped the killer's body with a strength that he had never experienced.

He let go of the cub who ran into a brook not far off to cool his scalding wounds. He trembled in terror every time his parents raged and roared in the outer dark. The wind carried the dust and odour of battle to his nostrils, making him dizzy.

Meanwhile, Bagni assailed her mate with uncontrollable anger. Her teeth seemed to crunch his neck-bone. With a cry of pain he exerted all his effort to tear himself away. Feeling that he was beaten, Bagni relaxed her grip. At once he disappeared in the jungle where he could soothe his aching wounds. Bagni made her way to the pool where Fierce-Face stood. After bathing herself and licking her son's wounds, she led him into a nearby hiding-place.

She, alone, had now to train her cub. There were many things Fierce-Face had to be taught before he could manage himself. First of all, to hunt by himself: The little tiger had to learn this before he was six months old.

~

One day his mother took him to a pool where pheasants drank. About sundown the pheasants came, splendid in carnelian and sapphire plumage.

The leader, the male of the covey, strutted up and down the shore of the white stream which purled like a child. The chief pheasant shrilly hooted. Two more males came, leading about eighteen females, all shining brass and russet red.

Bagni softly dug her claw into the cub's body. Instantly, he pressed his belly to the grass and set out crawling. He moved slowly with the noiselessness of a snake.

In the meantime the males took their drink, then stood by to protect, while the females drank their fill.

A dry leaf cracked as it was crushed under Fierce-Face. The pheasants made ready to fly up into the nearest tree. Suddenly, a terrific growl rent the air. The mother tiger's call had a double effect. The birds were puzzled and held their ground, while the little cub leaped and fell on their leader. Alas, he had only the tail of the pheasant in his grip. With a clamour of wings the leader and the whole covey escaped to the trees above.

The tigress ambled up to the side of her infant. Instead of thrashing him, she spent the rest of the day in teaching him to hunt. One, two, three, he leapt at her as if she were a rabbit. Each time she eluded him. This went on till sundown.

2
Training

Fierce-Face was an animal; he had to be educated to become a good one in the manner resembling that of a human child. The difference that marks the training of the young of the two species lies in this: A tiger is trained within the first fifteen months of his life, while men educate their offspring for years.

A kitten in a man's world is as ignorant of the art of eating as a tiger-cub in the jungle. Their mothers have to teach them everything. A tigress has to begin at the beginning: the cub has to be shown where the most tender part of a kill is located. Even then, the little one hurts his lips several times, for he tries to bite too near the hoof or horn of an antelope.

Though Fierce-Face bruised himself more than once by attempting to start a meal with the wrong part of a deer, his parent would do nothing to correct him. She let him suffer and learn. She knew that the example she set was important. Imitating her, he slowly formed the right habit. Gradually, he learnt to look for the belly and the throat of a kill.

How to eat properly is not so difficult. But hunting for a prey is most difficult. Any human being can be taught table-manners in a short time. It takes years to learn a craft by which he will win his daily bread. The art of hunting had to be mastered before the little one had passed his tenth month. Again and again the mother cat would lead Fierce-Face in sham charges against monkeys at the drinking place, herds of deer, and the nilgais. Each one of these served to destroy his sense of fear. Confidence took root in his mind.

Fear at first was his wisdom. Whatever felt unfamiliar made him hide. But with familiarity increased his desire to attack. After their first experience with nilgais, they set to attacking village cattle. In order to prove to him that tigers were superior in courage, the parent made a mock-attack. The cows had no bulls in the herd. For a bull fights back. In the present case, the very sight of Bagni made all the cows race home, their tails stabbing the sky.

It took several mock-hunts before the cub would banish fear. His terror rose from the feeling that he was tiny in size. A cow seemed very high, its eyes too large, and its horns bristled with menace. His last fear centred around elephants, towering high, swinging their trunks. Not only that, but his feet told him that the very ground trembles where an elephant walks. The earth quaked! The more he watched the big beasts, the deeper grew his respect for them. The ease with which elephants went in and out of the water strengthened his awe for them. As for their reach overhead, how could he measure it? Last of all, the care his family took to avoid them drove home the idea that the hathi is a kingly animal. No man can imagine how an elephant appears when seen through the eyes of a tiger-kitten.

Seeing a whole herd of hathis, suddenly abroad in the woods, he feels exposed, too exposed, to the eyes of the elephant. This is the reason for his fear. Tigers do not fear an elephant after they get acquainted with his habits. Only one animal is dreaded by them.

It is not a reptile; nor a bird. Nor is it man. It is the wild boar.

One day Fierce-Face was brought near a Horn-tooth. No sooner had the latter seen the cats than he charged. The mother roared and stood her ground. The pig, towering twice as high as she, came on. He had shut his eyes. He went by hearing. The ground trembled under his weight. His tusks flashed like crystal.

Imitating his mother, Fierce-Face, too, was facing the charge. Horn-tooth was within a dozen feet now, causing earthquakes. The quaking ground, instead of making him turn and run, roused Fierce-Face to reckless anger. A strange tremor ran through his body. Like an act in magic a mere cub became a male tiger. Suddenly, as if seized with a new will, he sprang at the enemy. He fell on the shoulder, digging his claws and teeth deep into the thick, harsh hair of the foe. The mother, having grasped the situation at a glance, leaped to his aid. She fell on the back of Horn-tooth with a sky-piercing howl.

About twice a hundred pounds of cat hitting him like a bolt made the boar slip. Instead of falling, he careered in a circle, then nosed the ground. The cats had already jumped off his back.

By the time he had braced himself for another charge, the two 'striped ones' were upon him… The boar died without inflicting on them any injury.

3

direction of growth

Along with hunting, Fierce-Face was taught to conquer his environment. No tiger lives in places he cannot rule. Either he must remain utterly fearless or move into new forests. The cats always make sure that both land and water are their own servants. Wild wood or land they master within a short time. It takes them a longer while to make sure of the rivers bordering it. In order to do this tigers are taught swimming.

This proved very painful for Fierce-Face. The cub was most unhappy about it. But his mother was unyielding. After finding all pushing and cuffing worse than useless, one sundown she took a decided step. Without hinting at what was about to happen, she led him to a wide stream, deep enough to come up to the nose of a cub.

There they both took a drink and rested. As if prompted by something unknown Bagni plunged into the water. It reached to her throat. But no higher. Without casting a single glance backward, she headed to the other bank. After shaking the water off her body, she mewed sweetly to her son.

His muscles stiffened. His eyes hardened. His tail trembled, then stiffened like a rod. Fear of the water, and of losing his mother were upon him. Just then he heard the loud snort of an animal from the rear. The tigress came back swiftly and pushed him into the stream, then started fording it with him.

This reminded him of the time when, hardly five weeks old, he was pushed into a shallow ravine to wash himself. There he rolled and screamed, till his own wits told him to walk to the shore. He remembered also this: how he had enjoyed being on dry ground once more.

At present he used his feet to feel the bed of the river carefully despite his mother's urging to move on rapidly. Hardly had he gone a quarter of the way through the water when he heard a few short but loud snorts. These and their echoes hitting the water stung him like arrows. Terror loosened his footing. He slipped. Here the water seemed too deep. He rolled and drifted downstream struggling with his outstretched paws.

A tiger opens his hand in order to strike. The little cat struck at the water. He repeated his stroke.

To his amazement he found that instead of killing the stream he was swimming on it…

The more he struck the liquid enemy, the easier seemed the task of floating. Bagni now came abreast of him and pushed forward.

When they had clambered up the far bank they looked back to identify the noises that had been drawing towards the river. It was like a thing of magic: there stood a wall of tusks, trunks, and heads of elephants, an entire herd! They had come to their drinking place as usual and were showing their resentment of all felines by trumpeting.

Swimming increased the cub's sense of self-confidence. He felt like a master—both on water and solid ground.

Now the female instructor set about weeding their entire jungle of dangerous cats and dogs; such as leopards, wolves, dogs and cheetahs. Single-handed she succeeded in scaring them away permanently.

Fierce-Face devoured these lessons. He took time to digest the idea that if other beasts of prey roamed in his world, they would eat all the bovine herds, leaving nothing for him.

4

drought-stricken land

Bagni went on teaching her cub. His final training lay in learning those feelings by which an animal knows remote dangers. Though remote, they are just as destructive as the attack by an enemy at hand. What are the remote dangers that threaten a tiger's life? They are fire, flood, drought and disease. A cat has to know them.

February was over. Mother and son moved into the neighborhood of man. In some parts of India it is the period of migration. From the first of March the dry season rules.

The present short spring ended in a heat wave.

First, it put its tentacles at the root of saplings, reeds, bamboo, and grass. Then, leaf by leaf the trees lost their brief spring foliage. The sudden burst of fragrance fell upon the land like a storm. Winter's decay was swept aside in a week.

In turn, spring was flung out of existence by the drought. Flowers withered as if poisoned. Leaves turned ashen on boughs. Dust like the finest powder descended layer upon layer on seeds and unborn herbs to hide them from the sun. That which yesterday was panoplied with spring now hid itself under a raiment of dust.

Such a crisis drives the wild ones in two directions. Some go to the depth of the jungle where thick branches of aged trees save the springs from completely drying up, while the rest of the forest-folk go to the land of wide rivers on whose banks men live.

'Civilization follows rivers.' The villages of India dot the banks of her immense streams. There seems to be an ancient understanding between men and beasts. They draw nearer each other oppressed by the common terror of drought bordering on famine. During this particular dry season, Fierce-Face met mankind; also a man-eating tiger.

This man-eater was about sixteen years old, past his

prime. His wind was poor. As for his muscles, they could not keep up a long chase after a wild animal of any kind. On the other hand, he had strength enough to pursue and kill domestic animals: such as cows, water buffaloes, sheep and goats. His powers were better than theirs. Every fibre of his body had been exercised, while they had lived their days at a slow pace.

It fell out that one day while he was chasing a cow, its herder stood in his way. The old cat was insane with anger. Without thinking, he chased and killed the wretched fellow. His easy victory over the unarmed biped convinced him that a man is easy to kill.

As the drought grew more and more relentless, bolder became the man-eater. In fact, he settled down to attack men and women and children. He had four legs to their two. He ran faster than they. Their two-footed run was no match for his speed.

The villagers found it dangerous to go out of doors after four in the afternoon. If there were some hardy spirits that did venture out, they left off doing so the moment they realized that there were two more tigers: Fierce-Face and his mother.

These two cats had come to the neighborhood of man indirectly; for they wanted to live near the broad river whose shores were ornamented with pasture, gardens and huts. The farmers who had seen the three cats thought them to be husband, wife and son! They hated the old murderer with good reason, but their hate of the other two was groundless.

In the meantime, the man-eater felt that the other cats had come to rob him of his single-handed reign of terror.

In order to feel safe, the villagers came to their parched fields with beat of drums, roar of trumpets, and lighted torches. The cringing bipeds had united their forces to meet the triple tiger-menace. No matter how brave, any tiger would run from the thunder of drums and swaying of a dozen torches.

Little Fierce-Face was disturbed. But not his mother. Her discipline grew harsher. She was determined to make a tiger out of him. His cub days must be ended. The rules that she had made had to be obeyed. She insisted on sleep by day and hunt by night. Besides, she refused her son's request to hunt man or his animals. She forced him to live by preying on the wild beasts that had drawn towards man's world of tawny rivers. It was not very easy to pursue many of these creatures, for there was no high grass to conceal the killer. Nor were there plants with leaves to give hiding quarters. In the moonlit hours the plains burnt with bright gold light betraying the movements of the smallest animals.

Yet mother and son disdained hurting man and his cattle. Once they killed a cow by mistake. It was a dark dusty night. By some chance the cowherds had forgotten a cow. This stupid animal had strayed far into the wilderness.

About midnight, Fierce-Face sighted on the bank of the river a crystal shape haloed with moonbeams. It struck awe into his heart. He had never seen a white cow roaming wild before. To him it was a divinity. His instinct urged him to sneak past this apparition of beauty. But something touched the tip of his tail. It was the paw of his guardian. She was saying, 'Attack, or I will strike you.'

He hesitated. Again that slight touch telegraphed to his brain, 'Attack or…'

Suddenly, the cow rose and groaned in anger. With horns ready, she came like a thunderbolt at the four sea-coloured eyes that she had seen. Fierce-Face was touched by terror. But that was nothing compared with the terrifying 'Grr' of his mother. It forced him to leap forward. The dusty moonlit air felt like sprays of topaz-coloured down.

At last he had done it! But the cow was too strong. With one shake of her body she threw him off her shoulder and plunged headlong at the mother. Alas, the tigress was an expert: she dodged by moving aside. Then she leaped at the cow, but missed. Apparently her intention was to make the cub do all the work. He seemed to sense this. He rushed after the fleeing prey roaring like a veteran of the game.

At this stage the bovine saw something that frightened her to a standstill. There was a third tiger standing in the distance. Stupidity, the proverbial quality of cows, led to her undoing. Instead of plunging at the man-eater, who had only come to look, she stopped to think. Before she had taken any decisive step, Fierce-Face was upon her neck.

The mother tiger watched, not her son but the old cat. He was already coming forward to share in the kill.

With a growl for a warning, she charged. The moonlight dripped from her body in silver rain. Claws and teeth began their deadly work. Howls of hate rolled on the river, then struck the sleeping houses and roofs.

In a few minutes the old fellow had learnt that it must be retreat or death. At this point he saw another tiger coming towards him. It was Fierce-Face bringing aid to his mother. This shook his self-confidence. A sharp blow seared his body. He rushed away into the jungle.

This battle led to the man-eater's capture by men. But we must tell the story event by event.

~

On the morrow, the old cat found himself bruised and cut in many places. Not only that, he had bled profusely through one wound. He was forced to heal himself. So he took to eating herbs. And these were not easy to find. Next he needed salt for his diet. Beasts of prey generally get salt from the meat and blood of their kill. He had no strength to get a victim. The only way left for him was to lick the mud of the river, for it was full of salty deposit. For days his diet consisted of mud and a few herbs. Owing to it he was not able to move fast or far.

A glance at the map of India will tell one that the Ganges reaches the sea in the Province of Bengal, the home of Royal Bengal tigers. There the water is full of crocodiles and the long fingers of land full of tigers. The holy river forks out into innumerable mud-red streams. Though the place rarely sees pythons, during the rains of August floods from the north wash down Himalayan serpents many feet long to the jungles of the salt lick. Once there, a tiger rarely forsakes the place. For to the long neck of land come many vegetarian animals to eat salt which prevents diseases such as dropsy. Here, at last, the civilized human beings found it easy to track the man-eater down. By watching from tree-tops, they made out the state of his health. Man's cunning worked faster than the animal's wisdom. They dug a pit ten feet deep and as many feet square, then covered it with bamboo and luscious twigs. To make it all the more innocent-looking they left a dozen roosters tethered to long strings on top. These crowed or ate grains of rice thrown down from a tree where a man hid. The latter had built a spacious platform where he kept sacks of food both for himself and for the decoys below. From his point of vantage he could see the movements of many animals on the floor of the jungle.

After several days spent in eating salty mud and grass, the man-eater felt very hungry. He needed diet fit for his race. His instinct told him to return to the village to hunt. This was difficult for one tired and worn. He felt hungrier and hungrier; every step that he took seemed to be his last.

It was about eleven in the morning when he was passing near the trap. He heard a rooster crow. He realized at once that it was a barnyard fowl. Thinking that he was drawing close to a village, he tried to hurry in the direction of the noise. He could not walk fast.

At this juncture he heard the roosters crow several times, and his ears told him that the birds were within reach. He ambled on laboriously. It was not long before he was standing near the trap. In the white heat haze caused by the tropical sun the yellow-red birds appeared like woodcocks of the wild. Deceptive colours hung in the air between the cat and the barnyard fowl. Just the same something within him hinted that he had better keep away.

From a tree-top a twig fell, hitting one of the birds. Its wings fluttered; then it screamed in pain. The man-eater surmised that all the birds might fly away, and he was too hungry to let this happen. So he rushed at the feathered fraternity. Then like a sleeper falling in his dreams, he fell—down and down and down…

Suddenly, he struck the bottom of the trap. Though the chickens had fallen with him, he had no desire to eat them. The catastrophe had robbed him of his appetite.

There he lay three days. Instead of killing him the villagers placed him in an iron cage and drove him to the nearest dealer in animals. After selling him, they took the proceeds home. It was distributed evenly among those whose cattle the man-eater had slain.

5

mystery of man

The village breathed easily after the caging of the old tiger. The latter, too, seemed relieved at the fact that he got one meal a day without the bother of hunting. Sometimes, homesick for the woods, he tried to break through his cage. But finding this futile, he resigned himself to captivity.

In the meantime, Fierce-Face with his mother's help began to study mankind. Day and night man engrossed his curiosity. The judgments formed on this subject he communicated to his mother for criticism.

One sundown after they had eaten off a wild pig, he said to his mother, 'Man is timid.'

The elder cat licked her paws clean, then remarked, 'But do not count on it. I have known him to run from cats in order to kill them by belching fire from up a tree. He is dangerous.'

'When is the beast most dangerous, mother?'

The old cat's eyes glowed with terror. She remarked, 'Do not come near man when on the neck of an elephant. He belches out unerring death-fire.'

'Why are elephants so stupid as to let man ride them?'

'Because Thick-Hide is a vegetarian, and like cattle and horse submits to man.'

'Tell me your experience with man on elephant, mother.'

'It was long, long ago, when your grandfather was killed. You see, all tom cats hate their sons. But they play with their daughters. I was hardly a year old when he and I were playing in a forest and we heard noises of elephants. These were the wild ones. They whispered through their trunks, "Man!" and ran silently out of sight. Then came two panthers; they, too, ran softly. Behind them came herd after herd of buffaloes mixed with deer in droves. Monkeys screamed from tree to tree as they ran. Parakeets, pigeons and peacocks screamed past. Now cats of all kinds: tigers, cheetahs and spotted leopards stole past. We caught their panic. My father nosed me from behind. We ran. We sprang over rivulets, thorn-patches, serpent holes and scorpion dens. These in turn imbibed our terror and hid out of sight. Now some monkeys jumped off their trees out of terror and joined the procession below.

'We came to an open space full of tall grass. There all the thud of our run was silenced instantly. Tame elephants with men on their necks faced us. Elephant and man atop. Sudden and puzzling! Between ourselves and the jungle beyond was an open space surrounded by man-elephants. Deer, buffalo and others were allowed to pass unhurt. But not cats. Any time we came into view, the lire fell on someone, killing him…

'Your grandfather said, "Follow me. I will frighten the man while you take advantage of his fear and run into the jungle opposite."

'We tigers never argue. I followed his order. He rushed the first elephant. In a trice he was almost on its neck. This made all the others trumpet and scatter. Without waiting to watch, I rushed past them into the jungle, some shots sizzling through the air after me.'

A dismal silence fell. The mother looked into the night glittering with fireflies. Fierce-Face asked, 'What happened to your father?'

'I never saw him again.'

6

man's weakness

Fierce-Face discovered man's greatest weakness by chance. One day a tethered elephant—tied to a tree—and a group of woodcutters saw him. The men instantly took refuge on the hathi. The latter usually brought them into the jungle, and at the end of the day carried loads of wood and some of the men back to their village. This spectacle puzzled Fierce-Face. In order to study it at a distance, he went under cover. Behold, the elephant would not move at all. The men had forgotten to cut his rope. When night came the tiger went off hunting. The men, finding their opportunity, freed their mount, then rode back to civilization.

The second time he saw men was at the drinking place. During the drought the need of water made the jungle folk and those of the village come to the one stream that had not dried up for water. Naturally, the need of it being great, every kind of hunting was suspended as if by common consent. Animals do not hold meetings and pass laws. They agree instinctively and carry out what seems to them universally desirable. From March till May they did not prey on one another near the river.

An antelope drank peacefully within twenty yards of a striped cat without becoming nervous. The code of the forest was adhered to by both… But when Fierce-Face came upon the men filling their bullock-skin water-jars with water, they dropped everything, and ran up the far shore. There they seemed to wander, making circles and emitting shouts. Fearing that they might do harm, he walked away to find Bagni. In the tiger language she informed her son that all animals walk in circles when very frightened. 'That is why tigers instinctively shrink from frightening each other.'

One day the tigress saw a cobra on her path. Behind her was her offspring. She did not want to go backwards lest it frighten the boy. To go forward meant death. She slouched, then lashed her tail. This told the one behind, 'Come abreast and do as I do.'

The cobra stood facing the tigress whose head was higher than his. It had not yet seen Fierce-Face who was hidden behind his parent, obeying silent messages.

It was a sight worthy of a painter. In the shadow of a leafless tree, between bronze reeds and grass, rose an ebony shape, growing longer every second. The sun played on its coil where a slight haze of dust wrought a veil. The tigress and the cub looked like brown rocks wearing jet-black cracks. Only when they moved they caused the dust to rise like amber. The cat in the lead had to crouch low or high according to the level kept by the enemy's eyes. Eye fought eye.

Slouching and swaying her head from side to side in time with the 'Stinger's' slow rhythm irked Bagni. But there was no other way of being safe. She must keep her eyes above those of her enemy by an inch. If the latter hissed, she snarled. Fortunately, they were not within striking distance of one another. Nor did they wish to draw nearer.

As if she had been struck a blow on the head, Bagni felt sleep, the most heavy sleep, come over her. That steady gazing down her nose had nearly hypnotized her. Snakes do not do this on purpose. But looking into their eyes steadily sometimes produces a weird effect on all animals. Desperate, though not outwitted, Bagni forced herself to lash the ground hard with her tail. It signalled the cub to come abreast of her. He came forward raising his head as high as he could. It stood higher than his parent's.

The snake felt dizzy when four tiger-eyes came into view. It tried to raise its head higher. This altered its angle of vision. Instantly, the hypnotic effect passed, giving the elder cat a fresh idea. She took several steps backwards, making Fierce-Face do the same.

The move had a strange effect on their enemy. A spasm passed through the creeping killer. The strain of watching two pairs of unrelenting topaz eyes had told on its sinuous spine. It could not stand erect any longer. Beaten and humbled, it slowly lowered its head and uncoiled itself. Resting and watching, it prepared to deal a fatal bite if attacked. But the cats made no move. Convinced that they meant to withdraw, the cobra slid out of sight.

7

a futile hunt

The drought had reached its final stage. Even the wildest animal sought shelter near humanity. Those buffaloes that keep far away from detection in the heart of the forest had stolen their way to the broad river.

One evening a black buffalo was seen grazing. It was a dark night. The bovine seemed to melt into the surrounding air. Now and then his muzzle touching the dry grass made the noise of small beads sliding on a string. Bagni hung back. Fierce-Face led the attack. He did all the formal moves as he had learnt, making a circle around his prey. The buffalo was so hungry that he kept busy eating, his nose close to the ground. The dust in the air obstructed his scenting the tiger. His nostrils signalled no danger, though the killer drew nearer by shortening the circle of attack. Still, no response from the grazer disconcerted Fierce-Face.

Crouching was the next thing to do: Pressing himself close to the ground, he advanced from the rear. He had taken care to come up the wind. Soon he was reaching the point whence a leap would land him on the buffalo's neck. Suddenly, something seemed to explode under his paw. A dry leaf crackled. The buffalo turned about and lowered his head. His tail stood erect, stabbing the sky. His eyes burnt scarlet.

The tigress saw it all from a nearby hiding place, but would not interfere. One misstep and she would be childless. Yet she would not break her silence. Crouching taut like a withe she watched. The buffalo bellowed as he ran forward. Fierce-Face being a male did what all males do when challenged. He roared: 'Gr-rr-!' The buffalo drew nearer and still nearer.

Like a bull-fighter the cat leapt away from his path. The horned one had anticipated this. He cut a short circle, fast as lightning, and plunged once more at the green eyes ahead. Again Fierce-Face dodged, alas, a shade too late. One horn had scratched his left haunch. The ensuing pain whetted his cunning to razor-edge. Instead of doing any tricks, he followed hot after the bull wherever he led. Invariably keeping close to its rear, he ran.

This fact, that he could not face his pursuer, worried the buffalo. He could not shake the fellow off his trail, nor could he see him in a cloud of dust. Feeling that he was free of his enemy behind the screen of dust, he ran in a straight line to the village.

The dogs who had been roused by the thud of his hoofs set up a howl rousing their owners from sleep. Lights began to flash from windows stinging his sight. The buffalo was frightened. His panic made him believe that he was flanked by tigers, men and dogs. His movements had to be carried out in a haze of dust, but it did not dull his nostrils. He could scent his way out into safety.

There was one point of the compass free of all odours of inimical beasts. It seemed free from danger. For a moment he slowed down in order to make sure of his bearings. He was appalled by what flashed ahead. A pair of green eyes peered through the dust thinned by a lazy wind. Instantly, he bent his neck and cast a swift glance backward. Another pair of burning emeralds was coming at him from behind. Stillness reigned everywhere. The dogs had stopped barking. Stillness and death were before him.

Suddenly he felt angry and rash. He rushed at the green image of death at the rear. This raised a cloud of dust screening him from the view of one feline killer at least. He plunged ahead with fury and force. So swiftly had he made his charge that he took the emerald eyes of Fierce-Face by thundering surprise. The dust that rose with the bull's passing seemed kindled with threats. Instead of running away Fierce-Face leaped for the bull's neck… And missed. In a trice the latter rushed to safety in the dry jungle.

8

where tigers die

That night passed without Bagni and Fierce-Face finding a morsel of food. A little before sunrise they decided to go into the deep forest for its coolness, for the sun seemed to burn every open space. The more they advanced, the thicker grew the shadow. Many trees, though nearly leafless, stretched their branches towards and into one another making a thick latticework through which the sun sent only a few of his deadly shafts.

The woods seemed deadlier than anything they had experienced so far. Not an animal disturbed the solitude of the place. Stillness lay heavy as lead on everything. They wandered without coming across a single prey. Yet, somewhat stimulated by the coolness, the cats pressed on. They trod carefully; not a dry leaf cracked under their pads, nor did the half-dead grass utter a swish. No dust rose from their track. There was nothing to indicate life.

At last they reached a spot where no sunlight fell through the drought-denuded boughs. The tree-trunks wore parched vines for a dress. Not a twig fell fretting the calmness of the region. Fierce-Face dared not suggest anything. He followed wherever his mother led. Now and then he would come abreast of her. Her eyes refused to speak to his. Yet she gazed at him with a feeling of assurance. Glance after glance said nothing more.

The elder cat's intuition told her of the nature of the place. Just the same her instinct drove her deeper into the homeland of lifelessness. The solitude that they traversed did not harbour even a scorpion. Not a spider stretched his hairy legs on a death-meshed web. No insect crawled. Not a fly buzzed. Only silence…which the two felines broke, though fearing to break it. Stillness, softer stillness, seemed to trammel their feet. Each muscle and every sinew felt the poison of desolation. Thus the lifeless life of the place haunted them. Death felt near, near enough to touch.

Suddenly the mother stopped. She mewed most gently. Fierce-Face stopped and looked... There were some bones under their feet. The parent cat mewed twice, thrice... Directed by her cry the young tiger glanced ahead. He saw a skeleton. Was this the burial place of the tigers?

During the drought several tigers had fallen exhausted during their march. And there they had lain down to their last sleep. The bones were not old. What could be the animal or animals that had lived on their flesh? These were the vultures of the air.

The two cats stole away from the place. Death seen face to face had purged from their nerves every form of desire. Even their hunger they could not feel.

One more night they spent without hunting. Though they had gone long marches and eaten nothing for several days, and though their nature was to keep awake through the dark hours, this night both fell asleep like kittens. The god of sleep erased from their brains most of the images of the sanctuary of death that they had gathered. This is Nature's way of curing nerves. Only animals and savages are the real masters of this cure.

9

conflagration

The drought ended in a forest fire. It was caused by wood-friction. The wind rubbed one dry branch of a tree against that of another forcing them both to smoke. Sparks falling from them set the dry brush on fire.

The buffaloes smelt it before it had spread. They mooed the news to the monkeys. The latter, in turn, screamed to the parakeets, wild martens, pheasants, kites, owls and ravens.

The song birds, whether *doel* (thrush), *papia* (nightingale) or the cooing doves fled to the highest summits of the air, too frightened to scream!

The first sign that the villagers caught of the danger was a fleet of flying peacocks. Squalls of sapphire and gold landed on housetops with the thud of stones. A cloud of white peacocks trailed by scarlet-russet pheasants descended on the mango-grove and the giant banyan, the only trees remaining green.

Among the four-footed nilgais and antelopes, herds of elephants skirted the village and vanished in the hot plains of India.

Not an animal was afraid of man now; the fear of fire had made all forget the lesser fear of mankind.

In the deep jungle another drama was enacted. Fierce-Face and his mother were cut off from the open fields by a curtain of smoke. Though behind them lay unlimited stretches of forest, yet the blaze before them had hypnotized them. Their one desire was to break through to the open fields. They hardly dreamt of running into the forest behind. Tigers like other animals think that man can conquer fire. At the slightest intimation of a blaze they run to the world of men. Apparently animals think man is master and maker of fire. For hundreds of years they have seen his houses belching smoke into the distant sky.

Fierce-Face led his mother from place to place

in search of an opening in the smoke-screen which might give them escape into the plough-lands.

The villagers in the meantime had carried everything they possessed on the backs of their animals to the broad river bank. Having made their families, chattels, etc., safe, they now banded themselves to save the village and the open fields from the jungle-flames. Soon a back-fire was started. It was when this back-fire was in progress that Fierce-Face decided to give up all attempts to go towards the village. The jungle was moving toward them, thronging with lighted torches. At this juncture the tigress took the lead. She set out for the hinterland behind them, dexterously skirting the homeland of death. They went for hours without meeting even the smallest animal. All the beasts had gone away from the burning forest.

They must have gone miles by now and reached the shallow bed of a wide river. It marked the end of one jungle and beginning of another. They walked past the middle to the cover of the high bank. There the water seemed two-span deep, and white, like the teeth of a boar. First they drank of it, then sprawled in its cooling silence.

'Protective colouring' hid them from both the

jungle afire and the woods beyond. Seen from the edge of the former they looked like russet-purple sand. To the animals in the woods nearby they seemed like black mud and withered reed. Instinct told mother and child that they were safe. Soothed by the water and overpowered by fatigue, they felt sleepy. Back to back they crouched, muzzles on paws. The water could not reach even their chins, it was so low.

About half an hour later the tigress heard something drop on the bank above. Then a silent expectancy seized her mind. It took her a long while to convince herself that nothing was the matter. When about ready to fall asleep again, she perceived that a thick, long stream of water was sliding down the embankment. It was an animal. A python! Instead of attacking her, it was approaching within a few yards of her sleeping child.

At this point Fierce-Face was shocked into wakefulness by a snort like screeching lightning passing over his head… Opening his eyes he saw a snake, very long and thick, approaching… Swifter than a bolt the tigress had fallen on its middle. For a while it became impossible to tell which was tiger, which was snake. Snarling and groaning she fought till the thumping of her paws had torn the serpent into ribbons.

This gave them a chance to feed their famished bodies.

How such a large snake came there was, and is, a mystery, for in most parts of India this type is not common. Generally it lives in the deepest part of the jungle where even cats do not go frequently.

In the present case, whether it had come to take a drink of water or to do harm we cannot guess. Probably it had fallen off the high bank as it had uncoiled itself from a tree and to its own amazement, found the two tigers below.

10
rainfall

Such is the life of wild cats. They eat when they can get food. Sometimes they march in the heat for days in quest of prey. At other times, they seem to hunt and dine every night. In exceptional times like drought or flood, they go without food without feeling hungry until they are far away from the zone of danger. It is true that with a sense of safety feelings of hunger and thirst attack the animals.

The fire that had consumed more than one forest was followed by a heavy rainfall. In the tropics Nature manifests extremes of weather. Bagni and Fierce-Face started on their way back to their home, the jungle that they had known intimately. The drops of water falling from above made travel easy, for they felt cool. Even the sounds of rain seemed cool.

The first drumming drops were followed by smaller ones breaking like glass globes on the leafless trees. Where there were dry leaves the water rattled like beads unstrung. But the most delectable sound came from the bed of the river...The showers were smothered in sand.

Hardly had the rain fallen than the ground blazed into leaping tongues of green. With the verdure came the animals that live on it. This solved the problem of hunger for all felines. Hunting became easy. Every two nights a barking deer, a sambur (the Indian elk) or a nilgai came the way of our friends. Life was bearable once more. In a week's time the forest became an emerald abyss full of life.

Males of some species have to declare war in order to win their mates. Love fights with death in order to win the one it loves. So now the two actors, Love and Death, resumed their ancient feud. Bulls bellowed, tigers roared, eagles screamed and staccato parakeets strung the air with their shrieks. Hidden rills came to life again. Springs that had seemed dead, now fiercely clawed their way out of the earth. When the sky had cleared, clamour of waters caressed the echoes from jungle to jungle.

If we were animals, we would find out that a knowledge of sounds is given to every youngling. In the case of elephants, whose eyes are not good, the science of noise and odours has to be given. To cats, sights and shades of sound are taught. Fierce-Face had learnt to grasp the meaning of many during his training. Even the fall of a leaf had to be gauged with clearness. He could tell whether the leaf was dry or wet by the manner of its striking the ground. If a serpent were sliding within a few yards, he surely knew it. Whether it was a panther or a large monkey moving in a tree above, he could decipher instantly. Elephants and boars or herds of wild cows were easy to discern from a distance, for the ground trembled under their march. Even the flight of flocks of geese he had no difficulty in guessing.

Insects, winds, grass and saplings baffled him. Though he could tell certainly whether a porcupine was bristling or not within a few paces, yet he could not quite see whether it was wind in the larches or a panther taking a slow drink. Here the evidence of the ear had to be verified by the eye. In time he learnt to do this quickly without errors.

11

the cub comes of age

It was not long before Fierce-Face had to face the supreme problem of his life. There appeared before him and his mother a tiger ten years old who seemed to be at the height of suppleness and energy. The way of his mother's meeting the intruder told the son that he must leave for her to marry him. Also in his blood he felt the call of mastery. He, too, must go and find his tigress. Instantly, he disappeared.

Though his mother looked for him here and there, she could not find him. Besides, her instinct told her that what had happened was right. Male cats hate one another intensely. Fierce-Face not only left his mother but he took good care not to come near the new tiger. He prowled and watched as he wandered away.

He had gone two days when he felt hungry enough to hunt alone. A tremor shook his body. He was indeed alone. Forlorn, friendless, he must seek out and kill his prey. How? It was not easy to hunt in a forest where the tall grass and thick leaves hid every animal from sight. Besides, his scent was not as keen as that of his prey. No feline animal has very sensitive nostrils. He has to use his eyes almost exclusively. Just now these were handicapped by the vegetation about him.

All day he roamed in vain. Searching after a stag proved useless and wearying. At sundown he went to a ravine and drank of its steaming, sun-possessed water. As evening stole through the jungle a wild boar, who had come to drink, saw him. He charged with a grunt that seemed to crack the tiger's hearing. The latter saw the white of tusks flash in the gloom. A moment more, these would go into his own throat. With a growl of disgust he leaped into the air and let the enemy pass under him. A low bough above got in his way. Instead of clearing the pig, he fell on its back clawing and biting.

This was wasting time. The enemy shook him off, but instead of running home, the stupid boar came at him once more. In the tiger's eyes there was death. In the blackness of night they glowed green framed in red rings. Fierce-Face struck at the hog's nose below his tusks making him roll on the ground. Like a hawk on a sparrow, he buried his teeth in his chest…

12

mating

To many tigers marriage is a lifelong relationship. It takes place after combats with a male or two. The young female has more than one suitor. Naturally, her husband has to humble them before she will permit herself to wed him.

Fierce-Face had not dreamt of marriage before he left his mother. In fact, many animals never think of it definitely. In the case of our tiger, he wanted a female to be his mother, for without her he felt lonely.

Thought is the harbinger of experience. In a few days he came upon a tigress about his own age. The dew was on the grass; wild flowers glowed scarlet and gold, while the sun rolled over the forest—a diamond wheel with spokes of ruby.

The female had just washed and dried herself clean of every trace of her hunt and gorging. On the water of the brook lay her shadow, a perfection of size and shape. About her rose tall grass and saplings, making a violet haze. Seen through it she seemed real and unreal at the same time.

Fierce-Face had come upon her without warning. She dug her paws into the ground in order to be ready for an attack. He, too, did the same. His eyes told him that this was a female. Now his ears heard a mewing sound. Responding to her with silence, he crouched and took his drink. A desire to show off came upon him. Instantly, he lay down by the water and licked himself clean. After he had finished his toilet, he looked up. Behold, there was no tigress!

But from that moment onward she watched him day and night. He failed to find her, but she never ceased following him. Lightly she moved about. He named her Light-Leap. Long before his decision, she had decided to marry him. Day by day she drew nearer. It soon became evident to him that he must look upon her as his mate. Animals do not delay in such matters: Fierce-Face became her friend and protector.

No sooner had she been seen playing with him than, one afternoon, a young male came from nowhere and set up a growl. Fierce-Face knew by instinct that this was a rival and he must fight for his lady. Hardly had Light-Leap withdrawn a dozen feet when the combat began.

It was not a fight between the feline and the bovine, nor did it resemble a war between panther and python. It was cat against cat for his mate. The jungle never sees more cruel or more cunning battle. The howl of these striped beasts silenced even the monkeys and the birds. The sunset sank softly as lead in water. Buffaloes, elephants and deer ran out of the remotest range of the roaring fighters. Night came clamorous with stars.

The battle stopped as suddenly as it had begun. Fierce-Face survived the struggle, the other did not. He panted, groaned and limped. Laboriously he dragged himself to a spring and lay in it.

Animals know by smell what the water carries. In some places the springs come through medicinal roots. They carry healing. Almost all the big game except the thick-skinned ones know this. When wounded and gashed they lie in the stream. They think the tongue of the water licks their wounds.

Fierce-Face lay on the lap of Mother Water till the 'belling' of a wild sambur announced dawn. He crawled into a dark shady place and fell asleep before sunrise. About midday he was roused by a purring noise. It was Light-Leap licking his wounds.

They hunted and played together until the end of another season of drought. About June when the rains had begun to pour incessantly Light-Leap gave her husband to understand that she was going to hide for the birth of her cubs. It is the law of tigers that they never should try to find out where the female goes for nearly three months.

HERE ENDS THE STORY
OF FIERCE-FACE

KARI
The Elephant

1

bringing up Kari

Kari, the elephant, was five months old when he was given to me to take care of. I was nine years old and I could reach his back if I stood on tiptoe. He seemed to remain that high for nearly two years. Perhaps we grew together; that is probably why I never found out just how tall he was. He lived in a pavilion, under a thatched roof which rested on thick tree stumps so that it could not fall in when Kari bumped against the poles as he moved about.

One of the first things Kari did was to save the life of a boy. Kari did not eat much but he nevertheless needed forty pounds of twigs a day to chew and play with. Every day I used to take him to the river in the morning for his bath. He would lie down on the sand bank while I rubbed him with the clean sand of the river for an hour. After that he would lie in the water for a long time. On coming out his skin would be shining like ebony, and he would squeal with pleasure as I rubbed water down his back. Then I would take him by the ear, because that is the easiest way to lead an elephant, and leave him on the edge of the jungle while I went into the forest to get some luscious twigs for his dinner. One has to have a very sharp hatchet to cut down these twigs; it takes half an hour to sharpen the hatchet because if a twig is mutilated an elephant will not touch it.

When one goes into the jungle, one must remember that there are laws one cannot break. Do you know that anyone who is afraid or who hates one of the animals of the jungle gives out an odour which attracts tigers and wolves? Every day that I was afraid to go into the jungle, I did not dare to stay on the ground for fear lest the tigers would smell my presence and attack me. I climbed a tree instead, because when one is in a tree the odour of one's body does not go into the forest, and the animals cannot tell whether one is afraid or not.

It was not an easy job, as you see, to get twigs and saplings for Kari. I had to climb all kinds of trees to get the most delicate and tender twigs. As he was very fond of the young branches of the banian tree which grows like a cathedral of leaves and branches, I was gathering some, one spring day in March, when I suddenly heard Kari calling to me in the distance. As he was still very young, the call was more like that of a baby than an elephant. I thought somebody was hurting him, so I came down from my tree and ran very fast to the edge of the forest where I had left him, but he was not there.

I looked all over, but I could not find him. I went near the edge of the water, and I saw a black something struggling above its surface. Then it rose higher and it was the trunk of my elephant. I thought he was drowning. I was helpless because I could not jump into the water and save his four hundred pounds since he was much higher than I. But I saw his back rise above the water and the moment he caught my eye, he began to trumpet and struggle up to the shore. Then, still trumpeting, he pushed me into the water and as I fell into the stream I saw a boy lying flat on the bottom of the river. He had not altogether touched bottom but was somewhat afloat. I came to the surface of the water to take my breath and there Kari was standing, his feet planted into the sand bank and his trunk stretched out like a hand waiting for mine. I dove down again and pulled the body of the drowning boy to the surface, but not being a good swimmer, I could not swim ashore and the slow current was already dragging me down. I clutched at reeds on the short but they broke and the weight of the boy was tiring out one hand while the other was already weak from excessive swimming and clutching at the reeds. Seeing us drift by in the current, Kari who was usually so slow and ponderous, suddenly darted down like a hawk and came halfway into the water where I saw him stretch out his trunk again. I raised up my hand to catch it and it slipped. I found myself going under the water again, but this time I found that the water was not very deep so I sank to the bottom of the river and doubled my feet under me and then suddenly kicked the river bed and so shot upwards like an arrow, in spite of the fact that I was holding the drowning boy with my hand. As my body rose above the water, I felt a lasso around my neck. This frightened me; I thought some water animal was going to swallow me. I heard the squealing of Kari, and I knew it was his trunk about my neck. He pulled us both ashore.

As the boy lay stretched on the ground I recognized the cowherd. He had gone to bathe in the river, had slipped too far out, and not knowing how to swim had almost been drowned. I put him flat on his face on the sand and the elephant put his trunk about his waist and lifted it gently up and down, and then up again. After doing this three or four times, the water began to come out of the boy's mouth and, not knowing what else to do because his body was cold, I slapped him very hard all over. After that I propped him up against the elephant's leg. Then the boy slowly came to.

In the meantime all his cows had wandered away in different directions. As I thought some had gone into the jungle, where I was afraid they might be eaten up by tigers, I sent Kari to bring them back to the river bank. But Kari got lost himself; so when the cowherd had recovered entirely, I went to look for his cows and my lost elephant. Where do you think I found him? He had gone right into the forest where I had left the saplings and the twigs and had buried his trunk into the heap and was eating the best of them, without any concern for the cows, the cowherd or myself.

But I could not punish him that day because he had done his duty by saving the life of the boy.

Kari was like a baby. He had to be trained to be good and if you did not tell him when he was naughty, he was up to more mischief than ever.

For instance, one day somebody gave him some bananas to eat. Very soon he developed a great love for ripe bananas. We used to keep large plates of fruit on a table near a window in the dining-room. One day all the bananas on that table disappeared and my family blamed the servants for eating all the fruit in the house. A few days later the fruit disappeared again; this time the blame was put on me, and I knew I had not done it. It made me very angry with my parents and the servants, for I was sure they had taken all the fruit. The next time the fruit disappeared, I found a banana all smashed up in Kari's pavilion. This surprised me very much, for I had never seen fruit there, and as you know, he had always lived on twigs.

Next day while I was sitting in the dining-room wondering whether I should take some fruit from the table without my parents' permission, a long, black thing, very much like a snake suddenly came through the window and disappeared with all the bananas. I was very much frightened because I had never seen snakes eat bananas and I thought it must be a terrible snake that would sneak in and take fruit. I crept out of the room and with great fear in my heart ran out of the house, feeling sure that the snake would come back into the house, eat all the fruit and kill all of us.

As I went out, I saw Kari's back disappearing in the direction of the pavilion and I was so frightened that I wanted his company to cheer me up. I ran after him into the pavilion and I found him there eating bananas. I stood still in astonishment; the bananas were lying strewn all around him. He stretched out his trunk and reached for one far away from where he was standing. That instant the trunk looked like a black snake, and I realized that Kari was the thief. I went to him, pulled him out by the ear and joyously showed my parents that it was Kari and not I that had eaten all the fruit these many weeks. Then I scolded him, for elephants understand words as well as children, and I said to him, 'Next time I see you stealing fruit, you will be whipped.' He knew that we were all angry with him, even the servants. His pride was so injured that he never stole another thing from the dining-room. And from then on, if anybody gave him any fruit, he always squealed as if to thank them.

An elephant is willing to be punished for having done wrong, but if you punish him without any reason, he will remember it and pay you back in your own coin.

Once I had taken him to bathe in the river; this was summer vacation and several boys came with me to help. Kari lay on the bank and we rubbed him all over with sand. Then he went into the water and most of us began to play. As Kari came up from the water, one of the boys, named Sudu, was standing on the bank. For no reason at all he hit the elephant three or four times with his whip. Kari squealed and ran away. I brought him home.

The next summer Kari had grown so big and fat that I could not reach his back even when I stood on tiptoe. We used to take him out wherever we went, sometimes one riding on his back, sometimes all walking along with him. We gave him luscious twigs if he behaved well and sometimes delicious fruit. Once in a great while as a special treat we would massage his chest with straw and he would squeal with joy and lie on his back as best he could with his fat legs, staring at the sun.

One day Sudu was standing on the river bank where I had just taken the elephant to give him his bath. That day Kari had been very good, so we prepared a straw massage for him. As it was very hot, however, we plunged into the river ourselves before giving him his bath, leaving Sudu and the elephant on the bank. Without warning, Kari rushed at him like a mad bull, threw his trunk about Sudu's neck, flung him into the water, and held him there for a long, long time. When Sudu was finally pulled out of the water and stretched on the ground, he was nearly senseless.

When Sudu asked me whether I would punish Kari for having disgraced him in public like that, I answered that the elephant was not rude. When Sudu asked me why, I said, 'Don't you remember about a year ago you whipped him for no reason at all, almost on the exact spot where he has just punished you?' Sudu felt so ashamed of himself that he got angry with all of us and went home alone. But by the next day, we had made up and the elephant had forgiven him. As a proof of friendship, when we went to the jungle on a picnic, Kari carried Sudu on his back. Since that day Sudu has never hurt a living creature.

An elephant must be taught when to sit down, when to walk, when to go fast, and when to go slow. You teach him these things as you teach a child. If you say 'Dhat' and pull him by the ear, he will gradually learn to sit down. Similarly, if you say 'Mali' and pull his trunk forward, he will gradually learn that that is the signal to walk.

Kari learned 'Mali' after three lessons, but it took him three weeks to learn 'Dhat'. He was no good at sitting down. And do you know why an elephant should be taught to sit down? Because he grows taller and taller than you who take care of him, so that when he is two or three years old, you can only reach his back with a ladder. It is, therefore, better to teach him to sit down by saying 'Dhat' so that you can climb upon his back, for who would want to carry a ladder around all the time?

The most difficult thing to teach an elephant is the master call. He generally takes five years to learn it properly. The master call is a strange hissing, howling sound, as if a snake and a tiger were fighting each other, and you have to make that kind of noise in his ear. And do you know what you expect an elephant to do when you give him the master call? If you are lost in the jungle and there is no way out, and everything is black except the stars above, you dare not stay very long anywhere. The only thing to do then is to give the master call and at once the elephant pulls down the tree in front of him with his trunk. This frightens all the animals away. As the tree comes crashing down, monkeys wake from their sleep and run from branch to branch—you can see them in the moonlight—and you can almost see the stags running in all directions below. You can hear the growl of the tiger in the distance. Even he is frightened. Then the elephant pulls down the next tree and the next, and the next. Soon you will find that he has made a road right through the jungle straight to your house.

2

how Kari saved our lives in the jungle

When Kari grew to be five years old, he was almost as high as the ceiling. He was never trained for hunting. We never thought of killing anything except snakes and tigers, and these we killed when they came toward the village and injured men. So Kari never had the training of a hunting elephant. Just the same, he was very alert and steady in the face of danger, so when it was a question of going into the jungle on the back of an elephant, we generally took Kari with us. During such trips we did not put a cloth of gold on his back or silver bells on his sides. These bells are made in certain parts of India where silversmiths know how to melt and mix silver so that when the clapper strikes the sides of the bell there will be a sound like rushing water. The two bells are tied by a silver chain and slung over the elephant's back, one dangling on each side of him. We never put a *howdah* on the back of Kari.

Do you know what a *howdah* is? It is a box with high sides inside of which there are chairs for travellers. The *howdahs* are generally for people who are not accustomed to elephants. They need the high sides so that when the elephant walks they will not fall from his back. They stay in their seats leaning on the edge of the box and see very little, especially children who are not tall enough to see over the sides. That is why Indian children prefer riding bareback on an elephant to taking a *howdah*.

One evening when my brother and I went out, we put a mattress on Kari's back and tied it very tightly with cords so that it would not slip, for it is not pleasant to slip and fall under an elephant's belly and be stepped on. But Kari was trained so that he would not have stepped on us even if we had slipped under him. We tightened the cords to the mattress, however, and lay down for the night. Though we had bells, we lifted them up and silenced the clappers, so that in walking through the jungle road they would not ring and frighten the animals, for the forest is the dwelling place of silence, and silence being the voice of God, no man dares to disturb it. We lay on the back of Kari and looked up at the stars. In India, the stars are so close that you can almost pluck them with your hands and the velvet blue of the sky is like a river of stillness running between banks of silver.

As we lay there, unable to go to sleep right away, we heard jungle sounds. The heavy tread of the elephant was like clouds brushing the crests of the forest. Once in a while you could see a tiger come out of the jungle, cross a road and disappear in the distance, but Kari was so brave he never condescended to notice the comings and goings of tigers. Once we heard the bark of a fox very near us and then he came out of the jungle. Kari stopped and the fox passed across the road, then we moved on again. In the moonlight, which made the road before us look like a river of silver, we saw squirrels leaping from branch to branch.

You know, perhaps, that elephants can sleep as they walk. Presently Kari's walk slackened into a slow pace, and we felt quite sure that he was dozing. Then we remembered nothing, for we too fell asleep. I cannot tell how much time passed before we were startled out of our sleep by a terrible roar, a ghastly trumpeting of the elephant and a terrible lunge of his body. We had to hold on to his back very tightly to avoid being thrown off. In a few seconds both of us had turned over—I do not know how—and were lying on our faces, holding on to the cords that held the mattress to Kari's back, while he broke into a run.

Trees bent and broke, branches fell, and we could hear the monkeys stampeding from tree to tree, and flocks of birds, startled out of their sleep, falling upon us, their wings beating our faces. We shouted to Kari to be calm, but he went on as if he were mad. We heard boars snorting, and running away, and strange-looking horned creatures leaping and bounding off in all directions. Then a tree in front of us fell, and the jungle throbbed for a moment. It seemed as though a shiver ran through Kari's body, and he stopped stock still. It was very difficult to tell exactly what had happened until we got off Kari's back. I spoke to him and he shook his head, then I spoke again and urged him to put up his head. He obeyed and I climbed down by his trunk. I felt it was very wet, however, and he shook me off with pain.

My brother spoke to me from above and said when I told him how the trunk felt, 'Now I know. You see, this is autumn when bears eat mahua in the moonlight under the thick shade of the trees. As you know, mahua intoxicates bears, and makes them sleepy. Some bear had fallen asleep under the trees and Kari, who was also asleep and consequently did not even smell him with his trunk, must have come upon him without suspecting his presence. Although all bears are brought up to respect elephants, this one, no doubt, was so sleepy that he did not know who was upon him and so I am sure he must have sprung up in his surprise and scratched Kari's trunk.'

If Kari had been wide awake he would have killed the bear, but being sleepy, the shock and the surprise of the attack and the pain in his trunk frightened him so that he ran out into the jungle mad with terror.

I put my hand on the trunk again. Yes, it was bleeding; I could see in the moonlight that it was not perspiration because my hand was dark red. I spoke to Kari again; this time he did not shake his head so furiously. He was rather willing to listen and I told him I was very sorry about his trunk but could do nothing here, I also told him to go back to the road. He shook his head—that meant 'No.' Do you know why he did not want to go back to that road? You shall learn at the end of this story.

I got upon his back again. 'Since he won't go back to the road,' said my brother, 'we must give him the master call so that he can make a road through the jungle' and we gave him the master call.

At this Kari lifted his bleeding trunk and smote down the first tree, and then he struck down the next tree. He came upon a third which his trunk could not pull down, so he turned around and walked away from it. After taking a few steps he stopped and slowly walked backwards and with one push of his back, knocked this tree down.

At this we could hear the flocks of birds flying in the air and feel the stamping feet below as herds of animals ran in every direction. We heard the vibrant jabber of monkeys from tree-tops, and each time a new tree fell there was more jabbering and more leaping away from tree to tree.

We clung to the elephant's back with our nails and teeth.

Soon we found ourselves on the road, three miles ahead of where Kari had been frightened by the bear.

Do you know why he did not go back to the same spot? Because no animal ever likes to return to the place where he lost his pride. For to be frightened is to lose one's pride.

3

Kari goes to town

When Kari was about five years old, another adventure befell him. We took him to see the town, but before we had started, we tried to train him to like dogs and monkeys. Elephants are proverbially irritated by dogs. When an elephant goes through a village, every dog barks at him, and while most elephants are too dignified to pay any attention, there are some who get extremely annoyed and try to chase the dogs. Sometimes, in fact, an elephant will chase a dog so hard that he will lose his way in the village.

Knowing that there were many unknown little

hamlets between our village and the city, we thought we would train Kari to like dogs before we started, for we did not want to be led astray into all sorts of little alleys while he chased the dogs who had annoyed him.

But as all the dogs of our village had seen Kari grow up they never paid any attention to him, and that made it all the more difficult to train Kari to like other dogs. He always thought the dogs in our little village were the right kind since they did not bark at him. Whenever a strange dog barked at him, he would chase the poor creature through the whole village and waste hours in finding his way back to the road.

We tried to train Kari by taking him to villages that he had not yet seen. There were no dogs in the first village we came to. We went through it without any trouble. In the second village we came across one or two dogs that barked a few times, then disappeared in the distance. Then, as we were leaving this village we heard terrible snorts and growls all around us and were suddenly surrounded by a pack of angry mongrels, curs and wild dogs. It was terrible to see Kari trying to chase them with his trunk. Sometimes he would try to step right on the back of a dog, but the dog would slip away from under him. Little by little as the dogs began to bark all around him, he started to go round and round in a circle, faster and faster till he was spinning like a top.

We had a hard time sitting on his back because we felt terribly dizzy. We were almost falling off, when we heard a piercing yell and saw the whole pack of tormentors running away. Kari had stepped on one of the dogs and killed it and that frightened the others away.

We then brought Kari home, gave him his bath in the river and offered him nice saplings and twigs, but he would eat none of them.

From that day on, Kari was never upset by the barking of dogs, but went through strange villages without paying any attention to them, no matter how hard they barked at his heels.

Now that he had become immune to dogs, we tried to make him like monkeys. Monkeys, as you know, are very annoying little creatures. I had a pet monkey of my own named Kopee, who was red-faced and tawny-coated. He never came near the elephant, and Kari never thought of going near him. Whenever we went out, this monkey used to sit on my shoulder, and if we passed through bazaars where mangoes and other fruits were sold, it was very difficult to keep Kopee from getting into mischief. In India everything is shown in the open, and the mangoes lie in baskets piled up one above the other like little hills. There were places where oranges were heaped up like big burning rocks. Here and there you could see brown men robed in white sitting near these mountains of fruit, bargaining about the prices.

Now it is very good to smell the fragrance of fruit, and one day while going through the lane of a village, as the fragrance of the fruit grew stronger, I forgot all about Kopee, and did not realize that I was carrying him on my shoulder.

Somehow the little monkey always knew when I was not thinking of him. At such moments he would invariably jump off my shoulder and run straight for the oranges or mangoes, take one or two of them and then make a dive for a sheltered spot. This upset the whole bazaar. Hundreds of men would pursue him from tree to tree, yelling and throwing stones till he vanished out of sight.

Of course, I used to get terribly frightened, fearing that the men would attack me for carrying such a mischievous monkey. I would hurry out of the bazaar and make for home as fast as I could go.

Then in an hour or two I would find Kopee on the house top, looking perfectly innocent and scratching himself. No one could ever tell by his face that he had stolen fruit a short while before.

When the time came for me to go to town, I was anxious to take Kopee and Kari with me, and I wanted the elephant to like the monkey and the monkey to behave like a gentleman toward the elephant. One day I brought the monkey on my shoulder and held him tight with both hands in front of the pavilion where the elephant was busy eating all kinds of saplings. Sometimes he would take a strong twig and unravel the top into a soft, fluffy tuft; then he would seize the other end of it with his trunk and brush himself. The moment he saw the monkey, he snorted and raised his trunk to grab him. With one wild scream the monkey jumped off my shoulder, climbed up the pavilion post and disappeared on the roof.

I went to Kari and spoke to him. I said, 'Kari, in order to like dogs you killed one, now don't kill my monkey in order to like monkeys.' He was very displeased that I should ever want him to like monkeys, because elephants are very much like some people who don't like to associate with others who have come from nowhere and whom they consider their inferiors. Elephants don't like to associate with monkeys, for they came from nowhere. You must remember, too, that elephants rarely see monkeys because monkeys are above the elephants most of the time, jumping and squealing among the trees in a manner most annoying to a quiet and sedate creature like an elephant.

It did not take more than a week, however, to bring Kari and Kopee together. One day there was a pile of fruit lying in the open, and the elephant stood at one end eating and the monkey at the other, both enjoying the feast. Of course, the elephant ate faster than the monkey, and realizing this, Kopee began to eat more quickly and soon had enormous pouches on each side of his face. Before long all the fruit was gone and the two animals were left facing each other. The monkey trembled with fear. He was almost on the point of running away to a tree-top, but, no one knows why, the elephant turned away from him and went into his pavilion. This gave the monkey great courage, so he went straight up to the roof of the pavilion, and peering down through the eaves, found out that the elephant lived on twigs and fruits and saplings just like himself. Having watched all this, I then got up on Kari's back and whistled to the monkey. He leaped down from the tree onto my shoulder. The elephant shivered for a moment and then was absolutely still. When I ordered him 'mali,' he walked on.

One day I took them to the bazaar, I on the elephant and the monkey on my shoulder. When we had reached a mountain of mangoes round the comer of a lane, the monkey jumped off and climbed up to the top of the pile. At this the owner of the fruit chased him away, yelling and shouting. The monkey climbed up the roof of a house, followed by a crowd. Kari, however, put out his trunk and helped himself to whatever fruits he liked, eating them with great relish. The moment he heard the people coming back from the monkey chase, he ran away—and you may be surprised to know that when an elephant runs, he can go more than ten miles an hour. By the time we reached home, Kopee had buried his face in an enormous mango and was covered with the juice.

At last we set off for the city, Kari and Kopee now the best of friends. It was very interesting at night going through the jungle country. The moonlight was intense, falling like white waters on the land. You could see the tree-tops, and at midnight almost clear down to the very floor of the jungle where the shadows were thick like packs of wolves crouching in sleep. The elephant went through these regions perfectly carefree. He did not care who came or went or what happened.

But not so the monkey. Monkeys, you know, are always afraid of snakes, and do you know why? Snakes go up trees and eat birds and their younglings. Monkeys also live by stealing eggs from different birds' nests. Now it sometimes happens that the snake eats all the birds' eggs in the nest and is resting there when the monkey puts his hands in to grab the eggs, so the monkey instead of getting the eggs is stung to death. As this sort of thing has been happening for thousands of years, it is natural that they fear snakes.

Monkeys also get punished for using their hands too much. Now, if you come across a snake, the best thing to do is not to touch it. Monkeys, however, accustomed to using their hands continually, grab a snake whenever they see one with the result that the snake usually stings them to death. I have never seen a snake do this, but I have seen dead snakes with marks on their bodies showing that monkeys had twisted them like ropes, broken their backs and thrown them down before the snakes could use their fangs. This, however, is very rare.

As we were going through the jungle that night, Kopee would shiver with terror whenever there was a swish of a snake's body in the grass below or in the leaves above, and I had to put my hand on his back and whisper, 'Don't be afraid, you are on the elephant's back and nothing can touch you.'

Another thing that used to frighten him was the hooting of the night owl. Any monkey that lives in the jungle is used to it, but as Kopee was born among human beings and had always lived with them, he had never heard jungle noises. When the owls beat their wings and gave the mating call and hoot, it was like a foam of noise rising over a river of silence. I, too, was alarmed when I would suddenly hear the hooting in my sleep, but both Kopee and I soon got used to it.

About four o'clock in the morning Kari stopped and refused to go a step further. Though I was asleep, Kopee began to pull me by the hand, and instantly after being aroused, I heard, or rather felt, as if clouds were passing by. The monkey's eyes were all eagerness and burning with excitement, and I looked down where he was looking. The honey-coloured moon was casting slanting rays into the jungle through dark moving clouds. We did not know what we saw. It seemed as though two or three hundred wild elephants in a herd were going through the jungle, or perhaps the clouds were feeding on the leaves that night. No one knows what it was, but we did know Silence walked by, telling us of the mysteries of the jungle, and we could not understand.

Then out of the stillness a bird's note fell through the jungle and there was a gleam of whiteness. That instant Silence was lifted, dawn began to sing through the jungle and you could hear its flute-like call fading away in the distance, followed by a momentary hush. Then the birds began to sing, and soon the sun came leaping over the forest like a horse of flame. This must have taken at least an hour and a half, but we did not even know when the elephant resumed his walk.

We soon came to a river where we stopped. I gave the elephant his bath. The monkey went off in search of food from tree to tree. Then I bathed myself and stood facing the East, saying these words of prayer:

'O Blossom of Eastern Silence,
Reveal to us the face of God,

Whose shadow is this day, and
Whose light is always within us.
Lead us from the unreal to the Real,
From sound into Silence,
From darkness unto Light, and
From death into Immortality.'

In India every hour has its prayer and every prayer can be said unconsciously anywhere. Nobody notices you if you kneel down on the road to say your prayer, in spite of the fact that you are blocking the traffic. Religion runs like singing waters by the shores of every human life in India.

I went to the forest nearby and got the elephant his food, and as he started to eat I began to cook my own meal. When travelling, it is better to cook one's own meal so that it will be dean and uncontaminated. Very soon I saw a caravan coming. Apparently Kopee had seen it from the tree-top as he was chattering with great excitement to tell me it was coming. I told him to hold his tongue because the elephant was getting restless.

I decided to go with the caravan into the town because the caravan people knew the shortest way. I also preferred to travel in human company rather than alone. No sooner had the caravan reached us than our attention was drawn to the faces of the camels probing the distance. You know how a camel examines the air as he goes along—he is continually stretching forth his head and smelling the air, and he can do this easily with his long neck. As camels live in the desert they must keep smelling the air to find out its humidity. Every time the air is very humid they know that water is nearby. That is why we call camels the examiners of space; in your country you would call them animal barometers.

The moment Kari saw the camels he snorted in anger, though the monkey was excited and thrilled. You see, elephants are the aristocrats of animals, while camels are snobs. You can easily tell a snob, he holds his head in a very supercilious way, always looking down on everyone, and don't you think if you put a monocle on a camel's eye he would look like any snob that walks down the avenue? Nevertheless, I made my elephant join the camels. That is to say, we kept about one hundred yards behind them because I could not let the monkey bound from camel hump to camel hump, and it would not do to let the elephant put his trunk about the camels' necks and twist them.

Toward midday the whole caravan stopped and all the animals were tied under different trees for two or three hours to rest. As we knew we could easily reach the city by sundown, we all enjoyed our siesta. About half-past three, the doves began to coo, and that made the monkey sit up and listen. Being a dweller of the trees by birth, Kopee was always sensitive to tree sounds. Soon a cuckoo called from the distance and in a few moments the caravan was ready to move on. Nothing exciting happened the rest of the journey.

4

Kari's adventure in Benares

As the sun went down in the gathering silence of the evening, we entered the city of Benares, the oldest city in India. For three thousand years stone has been laid on stone to keep this city with its haughty towers and sombre domes above the rushing and destroying currents of the sacred river. The river like a liquid axe is continually cutting away the foundations of the city. At night you can hear the whispering Ganges gnawing at the stone embankments. And that is why all the tall towers of Benares lean slightly over the water's edge. Their roots are being cut as beavers cut the roots of trees. And any Hindu who comes into Benares feels the age of India; she has lived very long—indeed too long, and it seems time no more clings to her than the morning dew clings to the lion's mane.

We went through Benares in a long, narrow file. The camels went first, and the monkey, who had jumped off my shoulder, was leaping from roof to roof following the tide of the caravan. Sometimes he would run ahead and chatter; and then suddenly disappear among roofs and walls. Then he would rush back to talk to me. I fastened two silver bells dangling from silver chains to the elephant's sides, and the cool sound of the bells sank into the cooler serenity of the Indian evening. People were walking about in purple and gold togas; on the house-tops were pigeons whose throats shone like iridescent beads. Through latticed balconies you could see the faces of women with eyes warm and tranquil as the midnight.

We had not gone very far when Kari put out his trunk and took a peacock fan out of a lady's hand as she leant against the railing of a balcony. He then proceeded to give it to me. I made him stop and give it back to its owner. The lady, however, would not take it. 'Oh, little dreamer of the evening,' she said, 'cool thyself with my peacock fan. Thy elephant is very wise, but I am afraid he is no worse a scamp than thou art.'

I took the fan, made my bow to the lady and went on. Hardly had we gone two more blocks when the screaming and jabbering monkey fell upon us. Behind him on the roof of one of the houses we saw a man with a long cudgel which he shook at the monkey. I stopped the elephant again and said to the man, 'Why art thou irate when the evening is so cool, little man of the city?'

'That monkey! Ten thousand curses upon him!' he said. 'He has been teasing my parrot in its cage, and has plucked so many of its feathers that it now looks like a beaked rat.'

'I shall indeed punish this wayward monkey,' I answered. 'But thou knowest that monkeys are no less wayward than thou and I.'

At this the man on the roof got very angry and began to hurl all kinds of abuses at me, but I prodded the elephant with my foot and he walked on, while the swearing and cursing of the little man of the city resounded in the stillness of the night. Nothing befell us that night as we took shelter in the open grounds outside of the city.

The following morning long before daybreak, I heard nothing but the beat, beat, beat of unknown feet on the dusky pavement of Benares. It seemed as though the stillness of the night were hurrying away. I left my animals where they were and went in quest of these beating feet. There is something sinister in this walk of the Indian. They walk with a great deal of poise, in fact, very much like an elephant, but also has the agility of the panther. I did not realize it until that early morning when I heard the moving feet, as one hears dogs on the hurrying heels of a stag.

Soon I reached the river bank where I saw thousands and thousands of pilgrims crowding the steps of the Ghaut, the staircase leading to the river, bathing and waiting to greet the dawn. As I followed their example and took my bath, there arose over the swaying crowd and the beating feet, a murmur like the spray of foam on the seashore after the breakers have dashed against the beach. Then the day broke like two horses of livid light rushing through the air. In the tropics the daybreak is very sudden. Hardly had those streaks of light spent themselves through the sky and over the waters, when a golden glow fell upon the faces of the people and they raised their hands in a gesture of benediction, greeting the morning sun which rose like a mountain of crimson under a tide of gold. All of us said our morning prayer, thousands of voices intoning together.

I could not stay at the Ghaut very long, however. I knew my animals would be looking for me, so I hastened back. Lo and behold, this sight greeted me! The monkey was sitting on the neck of the elephant, and Kari, who had never been accustomed to that sort of thing was running all around, raising his trunk and bending it backwards to reach the monkey in frantic efforts to shake him off. The one spot that an elephant cannot shake, however, is his neck, so the monkey stayed there perfectly calm, looking into space, secure in his seat.

I shouted to Kari to stop, and seeing me, he came rushing towards me, trembling. He made an effort to shake Kopee off, but the monkey was glued to his neck. I swore at Kopee and told him to get off. He looked down at me as if nothing had happened. I, too, was very irritated, for even I had never seen a monkey on an elephant's neck. That is considered very improper. I threw a stone at the monkey and he jumped from the elephant's neck, went straight up a tree and stayed there. I patted Kari's back and tried to soothe him. Then I took him by the ear and we walked into town.

Kari loved human beings; the more he saw them, the happier he felt. He glided by them like a human child. I was very proud of him and his behaviour. As we went on our way, a mouse ran out of a hole in the foundations of a house in front of us. Kari turned around, curled up his trunk, put it in his mouth and ran. You see elephants are not afraid of anything except mice, for a mouse can crawl into an elephant's trunk and disappear in his head. I was humiliated beyond measure at Kari's behaviour. He did not stop till he reached the open ground which we had left half an hour before. The monkey was still sitting in the tree. Seeing us, he shook a purse at me. He had stolen somebody's purse and was holding it in his hands waiting for it to be ransomed.

Monkeys are very much like bandits. Once, I remember, my little sister who was two months old, was lying in a basket on the veranda. Suddenly we heard her crying, and going out on the veranda found that she was not there. Basket and all had disappeared. Then we looked up at a tree and there was an enormous baboon looking down at us, while with one hand he held the basket, which was resting on a branch. My father, however, knew what to do. He sent a servant at once to the bazaar, and in the meantime brought all of the fruit in the house and spread it on the floor of the veranda. The monkey shook his head, meaning that was not ransom enough for him. Very soon the servant returned with an enormous quantity of bananas. The baboon immediately came down, and it was remarkable how he brought down the basket without upsetting it.

My mother, all this while, was weeping silently, leaning against the door. But now her grief was turned to gladness, for lo, and behold, there was the baby asleep in the basket on the veranda, while the baboon sat on a pile of bananas giving a strange monkey call to other monkeys.

Scarcely had we taken the baby into the house and shut the glass doors of the veranda, when we heard monkeys hooting and calling from all directions, leaping from tree to tree and falling with a great thud on our roof. In ten minutes the veranda became a regular parliament of monkeys chattering over their dinners. After this we were very careful about the baby. Every time she was put out, a man or woman with a stick always watched over her.

Remembering now what had happened to my sister years ago, I called to the men of the caravan who had not yet started and told them the monkey had the purse. True enough, one of them was accusing his servant of having stolen his purse. I told them to buy some bananas and leave them under the tree, and in the course of the day the monkey would come down, leave the purse and take the bananas. I had been humiliated by my elephant, and now being disgusted with my monkey, I took Kari into town again. This time I had my *ankus* with me, so that in case he should run away again I could prick his neck and make him behave.

We went by jewellers' shops where they were cutting diamonds, and stopped in front of the goldsmith's door. Seeing us wait there, the smith came out. 'What do you want, do you want gold rings for your elephant's tusks?' You know they put rings on elephant's tusks as human beings put gold in their teeth.

'His tusks have just begun to sprout; they're too beautiful to spoil with rings yet,' I answered.

'But my rings always make tusks more beautiful,' was his retort.

I answered, 'All the city folk think that what they do makes everything beautiful. Why don't they make their dirty city beautiful?'

The smith was angry. 'If thou be not a buyer of gold, nor a vendor of silver, tarry not at my door; I have no time for beggars.'

As we trotted off, I called back, 'I do not sell silver, nor do I buy gold, but when my elephant grows up, he will have such tusks that you will cast eyes of envy on them. But this elephant will live more than one hundred and twenty-five years and thou shalt be dead by then, and so there will be no chance of soiling his ivory by buying thy gold.'

We walked on very silently through the city, and then of a sudden a pack of dogs were upon us. We knew not whence they had come. Kari was as dignified as a mountain; he never noticed them, but the less attention he paid to them, the more audacious the dogs grew. They came after us and I did not know what to do, as I did not even have a stone to throw at them. In a few moments, we were hemmed in by packs of dogs. Quickly now, Kari turned round and in an instant lifted a dog into the air with his trunk. As the dog would have been dashed into bits, I yelled into his ear, 'Brother, brother, do not kill him, but let him down gently, he will not bite you.'

At this moment the dog gave such a terrible cry of pain as the trunk was coming down that Kari stopped and slowly brought him to the ground. The dog, however, was already dead; the pressure of the trunk had killed him, and the other dogs, seeing his fate, had run away.

Kari walked rapidly out of the city and I was heart-sick. He went straight to the river bank and with great difficulty walked down the steps of the Ghaut and buried all except his trunk in the water. He stood there knowing that I knew that he had done something wrong and he was trying to cleanse himself of it. I, too, took my bath.

Late in the afternoon, we went back and found Kopee still sitting on the same tree and looking for us, as the caravan had left long ago. Judging by the banana peels under the trees, we realized he had had his dinner. Kari and I, however, were very hungry and we were both sick of the city. We did not want to see it again, so I called to the monkey to follow and urged the elephant to go on to the nearest forest.

Kopee, with one leap, jumped on my neck as I sat on the elephant's back.

This ended Kari's expedition to the city. It is better for animals to be where the jungle is, for the jungle is sweeter and kinder than that wilderness of stones—the city.

5

the jungle spirit

It took us much longer to return home. We lost nearly twenty-four hours in a jungle where we had the strangest experiences of our lives. We had already covered half the distance when one day at noon we reached the river across which lay the jungle. It was so hot that Kari would not go any further. The moment he smelled the moist earth of the river bank, he literally ran into the water and lay there. Kopee and I had to sit on his back, while the waves of the river played around us as the waves of the sea play around an island. Kari kept his trunk above the water, and when he moved we almost fell off his back. The monkey clung to me, for, as you know, monkeys do not know how to swim. There are two reasons why monkeys are afraid of the water; not only are they unable to swim because the fingers of their hands are not webbed together as are ducks' toes, but being accustomed to go through the air by leaping from branch to branch, they think that they should leap from place to place in the water.

Seeing that the elephant was wayward, I told Kopee to hold on to my head. Then I swam ashore and waited for the elephant to come out. Now that we were off his back, he raised himself a little above the water and began to draw vast quantities of water up his trunk and snorted it out at the monkey who was running up and down the shore, chattering fiercely and keeping at a safe distance to avoid being drenched.

This shows that elephants have a sense of humour. They always know where to keep a monkey, and it is the monkey's business to know when the elephant is going to indulge in humour.

As elephants do not know that monkeys cannot swim, I was afraid that if Kopee was not careful, Kari might throw him into the river for fun, and that would have been the end of him.

I soon forgot the elephant and the monkey, however, and fell asleep on the river bank. I was awakened by a terrible cry from the monkey and a trumpeting from the elephant. I sat up with a start and I saw Kopee sitting on the ground shivering with terror, and Kari standing in front of him, waving his trunk in the air and trumpeting for all he was worth. I lay on the ground and lifted myself on my elbows. Through the elephant's legs I saw a great snake, right under him, held almost between his forelegs. My blood congealed in terror. Of course Kari was five years old; his skin was so thick that the cobra could never bite deep enough to bury its poisonous fangs in his arteries. The monkey was hypnotized with fear, but he could neither run away, nor go forward, nor come to me. He sat there shivering with terror.

I crept slyly around the elephant and approached Kopee. I knew that if I touched him, he would turn around and bite me. He was so frightened that anything that touched him would mean to his excited brain only the sting of the snake. The idea that he would be stung to death had taken possession of the whole animal.

I could now see what had happened. The elephant had stepped on the middle of the snake. Its back was broken and it could not move, but there was life in the rest of its body and it was standing erect like a sharp column of ebony, its black hood with a white mark on it spread out as large as the palm of a man's hand. Of course, it could not stay in that position long. It swayed and almost fell to the ground. The moment that happened, Kari raised his foot and put it down on the snake's neck. But the snake lifted up its head in such a way that whenever there was a chance for the elephant to put his foot on its head it would immediately raise itself on its broken back. Its agony must have been great, yet it would not give in for a long time.

As the snake could not move with its back broken and the foot of the elephant still on it, I knew I had better go and kill it with a stick. As I approached it with my stick, the monkey's eyes which had been fixed on the snake, suddenly moved. He looked at me and bounded off with a piercing, chattering yell towards the nearest tree. The spirit of terror that had held him hypnotized so long was broken at last, for he had seen someone who could kill the snake.

The moment the monkey bounded off, the snake stung the elephant's toe nails, those horny plates around his feet. This is a vital spot, as the arteries come very near the surface. Knowing this, Kari raised his foot. Evidently he was not hurt, but I was not sure how long he could stand on three legs. I was also afraid that he would fall and bring his trunk near the snake, and any snake can poison an elephant by stinging the end of his trunk. I hit the snake on the head with my stick, but instead of striking his head, the stick slipped down that ebony column which was still standing erect. Fortunately, in order to avert the next blow, the snake fell on his side. That very instant the up-raised foot of the elephant was on his head.

Kari walked away and pawed the sand with his feet to cleanse them. I thought of calling to Kopee who had taken refuge on a tree-top, but I was so anxious to know whether the elephant's foot was hurt or not, that I followed him about until he let me look at it. I was relieved to see that the skin of his foot had not been broken.

Then I called to the monkey to come down from the tree. He shook his head. I knew he was so ashamed of being afraid that he preferred to be alone in the privacy of the tree in order to gather his forces together.

The sun was beginning to sink. The jungle was not

very far off and I was certain that the breeze blowing across the river had taken the scent of human beings into the depths of the forest.

The twilight came swiftly. The bars of gold and light vibrated over the tawny waters, and darkness fell like a black sword, cutting the day from the night. The voices of the birds from the tree-tops, here and there died down, and as if to enhance the silence, insect voices came from under the grass. I got on my elephant's back and sat there quietly, for as the evening Silence goes by, each man must make his prayer. As the Silence walked on, I could see the grass waving in zig-zag curves across the river. It was always making half the figure eight in the undergrowth of the jungle.

Gradually all grew still and then over the river came the terrible hunger wail of a tiger. That instant its tawny face scarred with blade emerged from behind green leaves. He saw I was across the river. The tiger's body is marked with the same stripes and curves as he makes in the grass when he walks, and people in the jungle can always tell by the wave of the grass which animal has passed that way.

Throughout the countryside, wherever the echo of the wail was heard, a tension fell upon everything.

Even the saplings were tense, and you could almost hear the cracking of the muscles of the animals holding themselves together and watching which way the tiger would pass. It was as if the horn of the chase had sounded and blown; each one had to take to cover.

Night came on apace. I wanted to tie Kari to a big tree, but he refused to be tied up that night. He paced up and down the shore without making the slightest noise. Then he would suddenly stand still and stop the waving of his ears in order to listen very intently to shadows of songs that might be passing. I stayed on his back, intent on knowing what he was going to do. Soon, very soon, the river became silver-yellow and over the jungle a quickening silence throbbed from leaf to leaf.

Then swiftly the terrible face of the moon was upon us. Kari snorted and stepped backwards. I, too, was surprised because this was another moon, very rarely seen by men. It was the moon bringing the call of the summer to the jungle. It was the call for hunt and challenge, when elephants kill elephants to win their mates. And under the moon lay a great sinister figure like the terrible face of a dragon.

The July cloud was hovering in the distance,

and between the cloud-banks and the moon I saw strange things, as if throngs of white animals were going from sky to sky—I don't know why—no one ever knows. These are the spirits of the jungle, the dead ancestors of the animals now living.

Without warning, Kari now plunged into the river. I spoke to him, scratched his neck with the *ankus,* but he would not stop. He forded the river, at times almost drowning, and charged madly up the other shore, where we were lost in the darkness of leaves and vines. No moonlight fell on us, not even the knowledge that the moon was up could be vouched for in this thick blade place.

6

Kari's story

I cannot tell how many hours passed. I think I fell asleep, but perhaps I saw this waking—I cannot tell. Suddenly Kari's face changed. He moved his eyes forward, looked at me, and said:

'Brother, this is the night of the jungle and I want you to hear a tale that my mother told me when I was four months old, and still roaming in the jungle. That was a short time before she and I were captured by men. I was born near the foothills of the Himalayas, for the snow-covered mountains could be seen in the distance, but we elephants were so proud of our own height that we never bothered about the hills. I once asked my mother, "Why do tigers smell like this? Wherever a tiger goes, he brings a terrible stench with him." This is what she told me:

"'Every animal that lives in the jungle is born to one kind of food or another. He either eats meat or he lives on herbs and fruits. Those who eat herbs never hate or fear, but those who eat other animals are tainted with both. We elephants never fear anyone or hate anyone and that is why we exude no stench, but a tiger has to live by killing. In order to kill one must hate, and in order to hate one must fear, and those spirits that you see walking through the air have taught all animals the secret of the jungle.

"'Now the secret of the jungle is this—the animal that lives by killing is diseased. He carries a strange, festering sore within him and that poisons his whole blood. Wherever he goes the stench of that poison reaches other animals, and this mother of us all who loves tigers, as well as the antelopes they kill, is so wise that animals that kill must be branded so that their victims will be able to take shelter. For this reason wherever the tiger goes his stench precedes him, and knowing this the fox comes out of his little hole and calls through the jungle that the tiger is out. Hence, here in the night when the moonlight falls on the thickest gloom, following the plaintive cry, the cunning fox, the servant of our mother, threads its way through the jungle giving the warning to all animals."

'Very soon one sees the black form of a tiger moving in the moonlight without the slightest sound. He never attacks elephants. After he passes, the horrible smell of carnage grows less and less, and then another fox gives the call throughout the jungle, telling the animals that the tiger has passed.

'If on the morrow thou comest to the same spot where the tiger and fox have passed, thou shalt not find a trace of their coming and going for it is the law of the jungle that no animal leaves the mark of his foot or the stain of his presence on leaves or grass. The victims of the tiger dare not leave footprints for it will give away their whereabouts. The cheetah, the tiger, and even the wild cats who live by killing, leave no trace behind. And that is why the dwelling of men annoys me so; they cannot even raise their heads without disturbing the air.'

In my dream, I asked him, 'How did you live with your elephant mother in the jungle?' 'Our life was a playing and a toil,' he answered, 'but the toil was a playing, and the playing was a toil. When the leaves began to get crisp and coloured and the sun called us to the South, we would leave the foothills of the Himalayas and follow the sacred river bed through vast forest lanes, going further and further south. Time and again we would come to dwellings of men. How wretched are men! Wherever they go they murder trees and slaughter forests! And in these comings and goings, I saw strange things.

'One winter we came to jungles on the seashore where I saw crocodiles lying on the banks of the Delta in the daytime, with their mouths open and little birds going in and out of them, cleaning their teeth, and eating all the insects that poison their gums. It is a pity we elephants have no birds to clean our teeth. And, there too, even in the water you could smell animals that lived on other animals.

'When we travelled, the old male masters went first, then the children, then babies and the mothers, and in the rear all the maidens and young fathers. When we went to sleep at night, the old ones made a ring of tusks, within which the young maids and the males each made rings, and in that triple ring we children slept guarded by elephants and stars. In my sleep in the jungle I have seen elephant ghosts in the sky shaking their tusks of lightning, roaring in anger and battling with the moon. These elephants of the sky are our dead ancestors watching over us. You know, in the beginning, elephants ruled over all other animals, and hence, men and monkeys and snakes and tigers were created.'

'Who made the rhinoceros?' I asked in my dream.

'The rhinoceros,' Kari answered, 'is a wayward elephant. Once when our ancestors were making a very beautiful animal they fell asleep. They had already completed the thick hide and the small legs, when some malicious spirit completed the head and instead of putting a trunk put a horn on it, and that is why the rhinoceros goes through the jungle like a spirit of evil. Dost thou not hear him coming tonight? The trees are falling and the saplings are cracking. The rhinoceros is snorting. That is the way of his coming; wherever he goes he carries destruction before him and he is not afraid to leave a trail behind, for no animal could kill him and tigers do not want to kill him because they cannot get beyond his hide.'

That minute a tall tree fell in front of us and the raging rhinoceros went by.

'Why does he walk straight?' I said to Kari. 'Most animals do not.'

'Only the well-born go round,' Kari said. 'The ill-bred find the shortest road to everything.'

Just then there was a stillness in the jungle and from nowhere, like marching clouds, came herds of elephants, silent and slow. Above there was no light. A vast blackness had been spread over the stars and moon, and throughout the gloom beyond there was a singing and an eagerness.

'Go up the tree,' Kari said to me. 'I want to be rid of you tonight.'

Sleeping or dreaming—I do not know—I did his bidding and then saw Kari stand and give a call and the whole elephant herd stopped. I could understand everything they said; and when they looked at him some of the young elephants laughed, 'Look, he has the mark of a chain on his ankle; he bears the slavery of man.'

Kari raised his trunk and silenced their silly chatter by trumpeting. Then he said, 'I want a mate tonight. How many of you free-born want to test my strength?'

One of the young elephants said, 'How old are you?'

'There is no age to a hero,' answered Kari.

One of the elephants, the leader of the herd,

shook his head. 'We have amongst us younglings who have taught tigers humility; we have amongst us younglings who have broken hillocks with their fury, and pulled down the thickest trees of the jungle. So thou, man lover, temper thy speech to humility; it is not meet for thee to seek a bride amongst the free-born.'

Kari snorted and said, 'Give forth the challenge, I accept.' And one of the elephants with two small tusks just coming out of his mouth stood out from the herd and trumpeted. Kari stood and a quiver ran through his muscles and I could see his body throb. 'Don't be afraid,' I whispered to him. 'We have taught you the tale of man; he does not know it.'

He waved his trunk at me and then plunged into the other elephant. The whole herd stood around and watched the fight. In a few moments a young girl elephant stood apart from the herd, watching the fight, and I knew she was the prize of this battle. First they put their trunks together and bellowed. Then the two mountains of flesh bounded at each other as if hills were striking hills. As I have said before, Kari's tusks were not long enough to be of any use, so every time they crushed against each other Kari had to be very careful to avoid the other's tusks.

At last their trunks came together and their bodies were tightly pinioned. They looked like a great mountain spinning round and round. There was a pause and Kari rose on his hind legs and held his front legs up. That instant the wild elephant let go of his trunk and leapt to cut Kari's trunk with his tusks, but before he could do that, Kari struck him on the head and he went reeling into the distance. He would have fallen if he had not struck against a tree, and if an elephant falls, that is the end of the battle.

As Kari thought he had struck his opponent down, he stood there feeling victorious and I could see a shiver of relief going through his body. The other elephant, however, gauged the distance and came upon him again with great momentum. Before Kari realized what had happened, the elephant gored him with his tusks. Kari gave a painful yell, and walking backwards drew his neck from the tusks of his opponent. I could feel a quake go through him as a tree which has just been cut throbs before it falls.

The herd yelled, and shook their heads with great glee, whispering, 'We have won.' Then Kari began to walk in a circle. The other elephant did likewise and they faced each other. Now and then they would come close together; their trunks would strike each other, then they would separate and go around again.

By this time the sky was black and the livid tongue of the lightning flickered on the crest of the clouds. But the rumble of the thunder could not be heard because the two elephants were trumpeting so loudly.

Again they locked trunks and bodies and spun around. Quickly Kari released his trunk and stood aside, leaving the other elephant to go spinning against the herd. That instant Kari ran forward and struck the side of the other elephant, giving him a broad-side blow and throwing him on the ground. The herd scattered and a clamour of wonder spread from elephant to elephant. Kari rose on his hind legs and fell upon his opponent with his forefeet, as he started to rise. The oldest elephant said, 'It is done.' At this the herd slunk away slowly and the beaten elephant was seen no more.

The female who was waiting for the end of this battle came up to Kari and they put their trunks together. A deafening crash of thunder fell upon the forest and the lightning was striking trees far and near. A terrible deluge of rain came and blotted everything out of sight. I clung to the branch of my tree for fear I might be washed down to the ground. I do not know how long it rained. When I looked up, I could see that there was a white light above, but the rain was still falling on me. Then I realized that the foliage above my head was so thick that the raindrops were caught in it and were still coming down. I did not dare to go up further into the tree, for the branches were very slippery, so I stayed until every drop of water had fallen.

The moon set and I could hear all kinds of noises. Many animals were moving about. From the tree-top I heard the shaking of the coats of the monkey, and below on the ground I felt the heaving of hoofs on the wet grass. Then all this stopped and on the wet undergrowth again there was a movement like the zig-zag stripe of the tiger's skin.

Suddenly, there was a bark followed by a deafening roar and then the thud of a leaping body falling on the ground. The tiger had found his kill. You know the tiger has three different calls—the hunger wail which is like a terrible sound cutting the jungle with hate; then the snorting bark of the tiger which means that he is nearing his prey; and then through the stillness of the jungle, one hears his third call, the triumphant roar of the kill, which means that he has found his prey. This roar has a terrible effect on the victim; it paralyzes him with terror, and like a lightning flash, along with the roar, the tiger falls upon his prey. This is just what was happening now a short while before sunrise. The tiger growled now and then to announce that he had had his dinner and then other small animals came up and fell upon the prey after he had left it.

All the animals who had taken shelter in their lairs and holes during the rain were now beginning to come out. This morning there was no silence in the jungle; in the small hours all the animals were eager to get something to eat, so that by day-break they could go to sleep with something in their stomachs. When the dawn came, I saw Kari standing under the tree in the thick twilight under the foliage. I came down on the ground to find traces of the struggle of the night. The rain had washed it all away, but as I got up and touched Kari's neck, he winced and I knew that the marks he bore were the only testimony of the battle.

We went back across the river, and found Kopee there, wet and miserable. He was glad to get down from the tree and get on the elephant's back and feel the sunlight on his skin. I urged Kari to get him something to eat, but he would not hear of it, so we hastened back toward the village. On our way home, I verified the law of the jungle, for Kari had really developed a slight stench. You may say that it was the wound that gave the odour, but I do not think so. When he went to war and battled with another elephant, he must have hated as well as feared, and the smell of fear and hate was upon him. It took nearly a fortnight to wash the stench away from him, and you must remember that it was not the bathing in the water that did it. It was in the gentle care and friendship of the village that Kari gradually forgot to hate his enemy.

7

the tiger hunt

I have told you that Kari was not a hunting elephant. After that experience in the jungle, however, he seemed to be above all fear and surprise. On many occasions he showed such dignity and composure that one could not recognize in him the old, nervous beast. Apparently that battle with the wild elephant gave him such confidence in his own strength that from that time on no incident could surprise him.

You do not know what music can do for animals. If you took a flute and played certain tunes on it, all of the snakes would come out of their holes and dance to the music! There is supposed to be a kind of flower, like a sensitive plant, that can be put to sleep by the playing of a very delicate tune. I have seen with my own eyes how fond the deer are of music. Sometimes in the middle of the afternoon, if you stand on the edge of the forest and play your flute and slowly strike the notes which sound like the whistling call of the antelope, you will see a strange phenomenon. The deer generally bark, but they also give a whistling call.

As I was playing my flute one afternoon, I remember distinctly that nothing happened for a while. I stopped and tried another tune. I heard a strange rustle in the leaves of the small plants of the jungle; but nothing came of it. Again I changed my time and played on. This time even the leaves did not move, so I was sure my flute was not catching the ear of any animal. I was heartbroken. I had gone to test my knowledge of flute-playing, but I found out that I could not attract any animal.

It was getting late; the darkness of the jungle became thicker and thicker, though the April sun was still scorching the open meadow. At last in desperation, I tried my only remaining tune, not being very proficient on the flute. For a while nothing happened. I played so intently that I paid attention to nothing else and was greatly startled to hear a noise as if someone were pulling on a rope. I looked up and there was a stag whose nostrils were quivering with excitement as if he scented the music. His beautiful forked horns were caught up in a creeper hanging from a tree, from which he was trying to free himself. I kept on playing, but did not take my eyes from him. At last he freed himself from the vine, but a tendril still clung to his horns like a crown of green. He came nearer and stood still.

I kept on playing, and one by one more golden faces began to come out from behind the foliage of the jungle. The spotted fawn, the musk-deer, gazelles and antelopes, all seemed to answer the call of the music. I stopped playing. That instant a shiver went through the herd; the stag stamped his foot on the ground and as swiftly as the waving of a blade of grass in the breeze they all disappeared in the forest. I could feel in the distance the shiver of the undergrowth of grass and saplings indicating the way the animals had passed.

Knowing this power of music over animals, I wanted to train Kari and Kopee to follow the tunes of my flute. Kopee was such a monkey that I could not make him listen. Whenever I began to play the flute, he would go to sleep or run up a tree. Monkeys have no brains.

Kari, on the contrary, though much worse at first, was more sensible. He paid no attention to any tune that I played, but once in a while, I would strike a note that would make him stop still and listen, and I could tell by his manner that this tune went home. Those long fanning ears of his would stop waving and the restless trunk would be still for a moment. Unfortunately, the notes that really reached his soul were very few—I could hardly sustain them for more than a minute and a half. Weeks passed before I could get them back again.

One day after the battle with the wild elephant in the jungle, I took up the flute again and began to play for him. I tried many notes and chords. At last I could sustain the tones he liked for more than three minutes. By the end of August, I could make Kari listen to my music for ten minutes at a time. When another winter had passed and summer came again, I could really command him with my music. I could sit on his back, almost on his neck, and play the flute, never saying a word, and guide him for days and days.

This summer a very daring tiger visited our village. His head looked like a tower and his body was as large as that of an ox. At first he came in the night and killed oxen or buffaloes, but one night he killed a man, and after that he never killed anything but men, for the tiger is as fond of human meat as we are of chicken.

Our house was very near the jungle; all our windows were barred with iron. Nothing could go in or out through them except mosquitoes or flies. One evening I was sitting at my window at about eight o'clock. I heard the cry of the Fayu, the fox which goes ahead of the tiger, giving the warning call to all the other animals. Then, as the darkness that night was not very intense, I could see the fox go by. Soon I could actually inhale the odour of a tiger.

In a few moments an enormous black creature came and stood in front of the window. As he sat down, the call of the fox in the distance stopped. After a while the tiger stood up and walked toward the window. That instant, the fox in the distance began to call. I was very frightened, but as I wanted to see the tiger clearly, I lit a match. He was so frightened by the sight of fire that with one growl he bounded off.

After that the tiger took to coming early in the afternoons. One day about four o'clock, we saw him standing on a rock across the river, looking at the village. The river was very shallow, hardly five inches deep, but it was very broad and full of sand bars. He stood looking at the village and growling with great joy. In India the government does not allow the people to carry rifles of any sort, so whenever a tiger or a leopard makes a nuisance of himself around the village you generally have to send for a British official to come and kill him. Word was sent to the magistrate of our district. In a few days a chubby-faced Englishman appeared. In the Indian sun the red face of the Westerner looks even redder.

There are certain rules by which men hunt in India. You never shoot an animal weaker than yourself, and if you want to shoot a tiger or a leopard, you give it a warning. If you do not do so, you generally pay for it. After the British official appeared, I was allowed to take him on my elephant and go out in the open to show him that Kari was fit for hunting. He fired a number of shots and killed several birds. Kari, who had never heard a shot before, and whom everyone expected to be frightened, did not pay the slightest attention to all the clamour of flying bullets. He knew at heart he was the master of the jungle, and hence nothing could surprise him. It is said in India that the mark of a gentleman is that he is never surprised. That shows that Kari's ancestors were undoubtedly very gentle elephants.

After killing some more birds, the magistrate became quite convinced that Kari would do for the hunt, so one morning about four o'clock we started out. I sat almost on the neck of my elephant playing my flute, and the magistrate sat in the *howdah* which had been especially prepared for him, since he was not accustomed to riding elephants any other way. We crossed the river and went far into the jungle. Beaters had gone ahead in large groups to stir up the jungle from all directions. It was very difficult to go through the jungle with the *howdah* on the elephant's back; and we had to edge our way along between brandies and trees.

After riding for at least two hours, we came to an open space and it was agreed that the beaters should drive all the animals to this clearing. This morning the sunrise was full of noise and without any of the soft and delicate silences which usually mark day-break in the jungle. I felt quite out of humour and apparently Kari was bored to death. He kept on pulling at one twig after another with his trunk, nibbling and wasting everything. Our passenger did not know any language but English, and as I knew nothing of English at that time, we spoke very little and only by signs.

The first animals to come before us were a herd of antelopes which dashed towards us like burnt gold flashing through emerald water. After they had passed, a lull fell on the scene, which was soon broken by the grunt and snort of a rhinoceros. He rushed forward in a straight line, as usual, breaking and tearing everything. Kari averted his gaze because elephants are always irritated by the ostentatious bustle of a rhinoceros. Then, soon after him we saw a horned boar rushing like a black javelin through the air, followed by many animals, weasels and wild cats, and once in a while a cheetah with its spotted skin. They refused to come out in the open, however, but always went behind the screen of foliage and grass, for they had smelled the danger signal, man and elephant.

Every little while we heard a passionate and angry growl. When this sound reached our ears, the magistrate would sit up with his rifle to take aim. Then there would be a lull. Now we could hear the cry of the beaters in the distance coming nearer and nearer. Suddenly a herd of elephants passed. They made no noise and left no trace, but passed by like walking cathedrals.

Again the angry growl fell on the jungle, but this time it was ahead of us. The beaters cried out again close by, but all were silenced by the roar of the approaching tiger. With one bound he appeared in the clearing, but immediately disappeared again. We could see him passing from one bush to another; and when he stopped we caught a glimpse of his hind legs. Without any warning the magistrate fired and like a thunder bolt, the tiger leaped in front of the elephant with one roar. Kari reared; he walked backwards and stood with his back against a tree. The magistrate could not shoot at the tiger without sending a bullet through my head, so he had to wait.

Then with a leap the tiger was by the side of the elephant, so close to the *howdah* that there was not the distance of even a rifle between him and the magistrate. I stopped my flute playing to swear at the magistrate. I said, 'You brother of a pig; why did you not give him warning before you shot? Who has ever heard of killing an animal without seeing him face to face? Can you kill a tiger by breaking his hind leg with a bullet?'

The man was livid with terror. He had the rifle in his hand but the tiger was reaching over the *howdah* and stretching out his paw to get him. He did not know what to do. Kari shook himself with all his strength but he could not shake the tiger off. He trumpeted in great pain because the tiger's claws were cutting into his flesh. He raised his trunk, swayed his body and bounded against a tree behind him; but still the tiger could not be shaken off. The nearer the tiger's paw came, the more the magistrate tried to lean against the side of the *howdah.* Pretty soon he moved towards the elephant's rear, and thus readied a corner of the *howdah* which gave him almost as much space as the length of a rifle. I saw the eye of the tiger turn first red and then yellow, and heard the terrible snarl which he gives only when he is sure of his prey. The quality of the snarl is such that it paralyzes his victim.

Seeing that the Englishman could do nothing and feeling sure that he would be killed, I knew I had to do something. I stopped swearing and with one terrible yell gave the elephant the master call. He went forward and put his trunk around a very thick branch of a tree and pulled it down with a great crash. That instant the tiger looked at the direction from which the noise had come. His head was near me now, and he did not know whether to attack me or go back to his former prey. It seemed as if hours passed. I was petrified with terror, yet I knew that if I let my fright get possession of me, I would be killed. So I controlled myself. Kari was now trying to strike the tiger with this trunk, but he could not get at him.

Suddenly I realized that the Englishman not only had the rifle's length between him and the tiger but was raising the rifle to take aim. Knowing this, I took my flute and hit the tiger's knuckles with it. He came toward me with his paw outstretched and caught the shawl which was loosely tied around my waist. I was glad to hear it tear because he had just missed my flesh. That instant I saw the Englishman put the barrel of the rifle into the tiger's ear. All I remembered was hot blood spurting over my face. Kari was running away with all his might and did not stop until he had crossed the clearing and disappeared beyond the trees. He was not hurt, except that his side was torn here and there with superficial wounds. When the beaters came, I made the elephant kneel down. We both got off. The Englishman went to see how big the tiger was while I led Kari in quest of my broken flute. Toward sun-down when they had skinned the tiger, they found its length to be nine feet, not counting the tail.

8

Kari and the quicksand

Though elephants are very unselfish animals, they behave like human beings when brought to the last extremity. The following adventure will show you what I mean.

One day, Kari and Kopee and I went to the river bank to help pull a big barge up the river. The towmen could not pull the ropes hard enough to make progress against the current. All that they could do was to stand still without getting ahead at all. So word was sent on to us and we three went to help out. I harnessed Kari with the tow rope. It was very amusing, as he had never pulled a weight in his life.

At first he pulled very hard. The rope almost broke and the barge swayed in the water, almost toppled, and then drifted to its previous position. The swift current was going against it and the people in the barge were shaking their hands and swearing at us as they were afraid that the vessel would capsize.

Kari did not care. After he had pulled the barge about two hundred yards he stopped; the rope slackened and then the current pulled against us. The rope became taut again and the men shrieked from the barge. When you tug a boat, you must not jerk at the rope but pull it gently, so I urged Kari to pull it smoothly. In the course of an hour, he had actually drawn the boat in, and at the end of our journey he had learned to pull evenly.

After that we went on playing on the river bank. Kopee jumped off the elephant's back and ran along the shore. I urged Kari to follow him, and as we kept on going, I lost all sense of direction and trusted to the intelligence of the animals. The monkey, however, had led us into a trap. We had run into quicksand and Kari began to sink. Every time he tried to lift his feet he seemed to go deeper into the mud and he was so frightened that he tried to take hold of the monkey with his trunk and step on him as something solid, but Kopee chattered and rushed up a tree.

Then Kari swung his trunk around, pulled down the mattress from his back, and putting it on the ground tried to step on it. That did not help, so he curled up his trunk behind to try to get me to step on. Each time he made an effort like that, however, he sank deeper into the mud. I saw the trunk curling back and creeping up to me like a python crawling up a hillside to coil around its prey. There was no more trumpeting or calling from the elephant, but a sinister silence through which he was trying to reach me. He had come to the end of his unselfishness. In order to save himself, he was willing to step on me.

The monkey screamed from the tree-top and I, jumping off the elephant's back, fell on the ground and ran. Kari kept on trumpeting and calling for help, and by this time he was chest deep in the mud. The rear of him had not sunk so far, so he was on a slant which made it all the more difficult for him to lift himself.

I ran off to the village and called for help. By the time we got back with ropes and planks, he was holding his trunk up in order to breathe, as the mud was up to his chin. There was only one thing to do, and that was to lift Kari by his own weight, so we tied the rope to the tree and flung it to him. He got it with his trunk and pulled. The rope throbbed and sang like an electric wire and the tree groaned with the tension, but all that happened was that the elephant slipped forward a little and his hind legs fell deeper into the mud.

Now he was perfectly flat in quicksand. But something very interesting had taken place. Now that he was holding on to the rope with all his mortal strength we knew that he would not let go of it, so it was easy to go near him and put planks under him, as the hind part of his belly had not yet sunk to the level of the mud. At last he stopped sinking, but as we could not put the planks under his feet it only meant that he would not go further down and smother to death.

Now that his head was lifted and there was an opening between him and the mud, the question was how to lift the front part of his body so that he could drag the rest of it out. Another elephant had to be called in. It turned out to be Kari's mother who had been given to the neighbouring king. By the time she arrived, however, dusk had fallen and nothing could be done. We trusted to God and left him to his quicksand for the night.

The next morning we found Kari in the same position as the previous evening. He had relaxed his hold on the rope but had not sunk deeper. We had to put more planks all around him but he now knew that he should not attack anyone because we were trying to save him. After the planks had been tested, his mother went up to him. She put her trunk around his neck and started to lift him, but he groaned with pain for he was being smothered. He began to sink again and we just had time to put some more planks between his chest and the mud.

We had also slipped a rope under him, which some men in a boat near the river bank came up and threw over his back. The hawser was made into a loop around his body and the other end was tied around the mother. Then she pulled with all her might, and her strength was so great that his fore-quarters were lifted up and his small legs dangled in the air. He was pulled forward quite a distance, when the hawser broke and his fore-legs fell on the plank. His hind legs now were sinking and we were terribly frightened. We felt as if we had lost him again.

The situation was not so bad as we thought,

however, as it was very easy to slip another hawser under him. This time we made a double loop around him, and also made him hold on to the rope around the tree with his trunk. He was very tired, but I urged him to obey me. And now with the aid of his mother, he managed to lift the rear half of his body and put first one leg and then the other on the plank. A great shout of joy went through the crowd as Kari walked on to solid ground. That instant the monkey jumped down from the tree and fell on Kari's neck; he was very glad to see his friend safe again. But Kari was in no humour for anyone's caresses and he shook Kopee off. The first thing I did was to pull some branches from a tree which Kari devoured hungrily. A hungry elephant is not to be bothered by anyone.

I had learned my lesson. I would no longer take my elephant anywhere and everywhere at the behest of the monkey, for monkeys have no judgment.

9
Kari's travels

Sometimes Kari was used for travel. He and I went through many distant places in India with camel caravans, carrying loads of silver and gold, spices and fruits. They went from one end of India to the other, passing through hot and deserted cities while our accustomed way when not in their company led through populous places and thick jungle regions. Elephants have an advantage over camels in this respect—gangs of robbers may attack a camel and his driver and rob him, but no one dares to attack an elephant. As the animals of the jungle do not care to touch an elephant, neither do wild men in desolate places. For this reason they generally used Kari when they wanted to send pearls and other jewels from one place to another.

Once, we were given the king's emerald to carry. It was as big as the morning star, and burned when the glow of the noon-day sun was upon it. Two epics were carved on it— on one side was the story of the heroes, and on the other the story of the gods. We left the city and passed into the jungle. Night came on apace and we stopped.

That night I watched the jungle as I had never watched it before. It was about nine o'clock; everything was dark and the stars were right on the tips of the trees. Below us in the foliage the eyes of the jungle were looking upon us. Wherever I turned, I thought I saw eyes. Kari swayed slightly from side to side and fell into a doze. The first thing that I noticed was the faint call of a night bird. When that died down, the hooting owl took it up. Then it passed into the soft wings of the bats and came into the leaves, and you could feel that noise shimmering down the trees like water in a dream till, with gentle undulations, it disappeared into the ground. The wild boar could be heard grazing. Then there was silence again.

Out of the blackness then came the green eyes of the wild cat below me and, as my eyes became more accustomed to the darkness, I saw small, beaver-like animals burrowing their way through leaves and brushes. I thought I saw weasels way below, and in the distance I felt the stag disturbing the leaves of small plants. Then there was a snarl in the jungle and these gently moving sounds and quivers ceased. An aching silence came over everything, broken only by strange insect voices like the spurting of water. Very soon the call of the fox was heard, and then the groan of the tiger, but that passed. As I was above the ground the odour of my breath went up in the air, and the animals never knew there was man about. Men always disturb animals because they hate and fear more than the animals.

Little by little the sounds died down and stillness took possession of the jungle. I saw herds of elephants go into the water to bathe. They did not make the slightest sound; their bodies sank into the water as clouds dip into the sunset. I could see them curling their trunks around their mates and plucking lilies from the water to eat. As the moon with its shadowy light had risen, I seemed to be looking at them through a veil of water. Close to the shore were the little ones stepping into the water and learning how to breathe quantities of water into their trunks and then snort it out slowly without the slightest sound. Soon their bath was over, but the only way you could tell that they had bathed was by hearing drops of water like twinkling stars fall from their wet bodies and strike the leaves on the ground.

This proved too much for Kari; he wanted to follow them. I had a hard time keeping him away from the herd, and despite all my urging, he ran right into the river. His mattress and everything that was tied to his back was wet through and through and I had to swim ashore. If the emerald had not been tied to my neck, it would have been lost in the water. I went up a tree and waited for Kari to come out of the water.

After I had sat on a branch a little while, I saw two stony eyes watching me. I looked, and looked and looked; a cold shiver ran up and down my back, but I was determined not to fear and hate. I made myself feel very brave and I stared right back into the shining eyes. They closed. In the moonlight I could distinctly see the head of a cobra lying on another branch very near mine. I had disturbed him going up. I knew if I moved a little he would get up and sting me to death, so I sat very still.

Soon there was a terrible hooting and wailing in the jungle. I heard hoofs stampeding in the distance. The noise grew louder and louder and I could feel a vast warm tongue licking the cool silence of the night. Then the cobra crawled along the branch to the trunk of the tree, and then on down to the ground. I, who was holding to the trunk, had to sit still while his cold body passed over my finger. But I was determined not to fear and I could feel the silken coolness passing over my hot hand. In an instant he was gone.

Now I caught sight of Kari snorting before me. As I knew something had taken possession of the jungle, I jumped on his back. While we hurried along we heard the whining snarl of a tiger, not the call of hate or killing, but the call for protection, swiftly following our lead. Being civilized, we instinctively knew the way out of the jungle to human habitation. We approached the village which was still sleeping in the morning greyness, and behind us saw deer, leopards, and wild cats rushing after us. Then the boars came after us, dashing out of the jungle in terror. Vast clouds of blackness were rising from the horizon, and when the morning light grew more intense, I realized they were clouds of smoke. The morning breeze was warm and in a short time the smell of burning leaves reached me. The forest was on fire.

We arrived at the village in an hour and a half. The sun was already up. The leopards came and sat near the houses as guileless as children; the boars snorted and ran into the rice fields to hide. The tiger came and sat in the open and watched the forest. The antelopes and the deer stood in the ponds and on the banks of the river. By instinct they knew that the water was the only place where the fire could not reach them. We saw flocks of birds flying to shelter. Soon we saw the red tongue of fire licking the grass and the trees. A terrible heat settled upon the countryside.

I could now go near any animal and touch him. The terrible danger which was common to all had made them forget their relations with each other—that of hunter and prey. Tiger, elephant and man were standing near each other. All had a sense of common friendship, as if the tiger had thrown away his stripes, man his fear, and the deer his sense of danger. We all looked at one another, brothers in a common bond of soul relationship. This sight made me realize why the Hindus believe that each plant and each animal, like man, has a golden thread of spirituality in its soul. In the darkness of the animal's eyes and the eloquence of man's mind it was the same Spirit, the great active Silence moving from life to life.

The jungle was burning to cinders. The tiger hid his face between his paws; the wild cats curled up, hiding their faces. None wanted to see the passing of the terror. Later in the afternoon some of the birds that were flying aimlessly around were drawn by the hypnotism of the flames into the jungle where they perished. If one is frightened beyond his control, fear possesses him so that he loses all consciousness of self-protection and he is drawn down into the vortex of the very destruction which rouses that fear.

The more I watched Kari and the other animals, the more I came to understand why Kari and I loved each other. We had a soul in common. I played the flute for him and was deeply moved. I felt that if I could be dumb like he, I could understand him better. This was the lesson the fire taught me: do not hate and fear animals. In them is the soul that is God, as it is also in us. Behind each face, human or animal, is the face of the Christ. Those who have eyes to see can always find it.

10

Kari in the lumber yard

Not long after this Kari was sent to the lumber yards. It was very interesting to see that he learned all the tricks of the lumber trade in a few days. He would pull heavy logs out of the forest into the open, lift the lighter ones with his trunk and pile than up, one on top of the other. He had such a good sense of symmetry that his piles were always extremely neat.

Soon an older elephant came to help him. Whenever there was a log which was too heavy for Kari to lift, they would each take one end of it and lift it on the lumber wagon. An elephant, as you see, can do the work of a truck.

We had reached a stage in the history of the world when motor engines did a large part of the work of the jungle. The elephants would bring the lumber from the forest and deposit it near these engines where it would be cut into proper lengths and then thrown out again to be piled up by the elephants.

The mechanics who ran these engines ate meat and drank liquor. It is very strange that when Western people come to the East, they do not give up their expensive ways of living. Drinking wine and eating meat is one thing in cold climates, where one has to keep warm, but in a hot climate a man is sure to go to pieces if he eats and drinks much. Kari had no objection to wine drinking, but he did not like meat-eating men any more than he liked meat-eating tigers. He never hated them or feared them, simply he somehow did not enjoy their company. But these white engineers who came from afar did not know that an elephant had a soul.

Kari always woke up at half past five and then went to work. Toward noon I would bathe him and put him in his shed. Early in the afternoon he would begin to work again. Later on he ate lots of rice of which he was very fond. In the evening I would tie him up in his shed while I went to sleep on a hammock outside.

One night, I heard a terrible trumpeting. I jumped down from my hammock and went into Kari's shed, where I found two drunken engineers lighting matches and throwing them at him. Kari, who was afraid of fire, as all animals are, was trumpeting angrily. I protested to the men, but they were so drunk that they only swore at me and went on flinging matches. Seeing that there was nothing else to do, I loosened all his chains except one, and let him stay there tied to the ground by one foot only.

An elephant's chain is generally driven about five or six feet into the ground and is then covered with cement and earth. An elephant can rarely break this kind of chain, but I was afraid that the matches might set the shed on fire, and I trusted Kari more than drunken men. I knew that if the shed caught fire the elephant could break one chain if he tried hard to escape. The night passed without any further incident, however.

I must explain why animals are afraid of fire. Fire, you see, is the one thing that they can never fight. They are not afraid of water, as most of them can swim, but if they are caught in fire, they are generally burned to death. For this reason they have built up a protective instinct against fire. Whenever there is fire of any sort, they run. As they have seen the jungle set on fire from time to time for generations and generations, the sight of fire frightens them more than anything else. As long as they have inherited this fear from their ancestors, it is very wise not to play with fire in the presence of animals. If an animal as powerful as an elephant were frightened by fire, he would run mad and do the greatest amount of mischief.

One noon when we had suspended work for the day, I tied Kari in his shed and lay down in my hammock to rest. Toward late afternoon, I heard the same terrible trumpeting that I had heard before. The same thing had happened again. The two engineers, being idle, had drunk liquor and were trying to tease the animals nearby. The shed had a thatched roof of straw. The walls were of clay, but there was a lot of bamboo lying on the floor. Kari was eating twigs, some of which happened to have dry leaves.

I came up to the elephant, and seeing what was going on, told the white men to stop teasing him. They would not hear of it, however. Just then I saw a flame rising from the leaves. Kari raised his trunk and trumpeted fiercely. As I was afraid that he would be burned to death, I hastened to loosen his chain and with one terrible trumpet he rushed out of the shed, trampling down one of the drunken men and killing him instantly. Kari then trumpeted more and more loudly, waving his trunk and rushing madly around.

Realizing the danger we were in, I went up a very heavy banian tree out of Kari's reach and lay among the leaves. The first thing he did was to go and put his foot on the automobile of the chief engineer, which happened to be standing outside of the shed. In a few minutes there was nothing but a mass of twisted steel on the ground, over which the elephant danced in anger. Then he saw the chief engineer and two other men standing on the porch of a bungalow. He rushed at them, but they knew what it meant to have a mad elephant about, and ran into the house. Kari then pulled down part of the thatched roof of the bungalow with his trunk, and finding no one there made straight for two new trucks that had only been in use a fortnight and broke them to pieces. Then he rushed at a bull which was grazing in a field, and wound his trunk around his neck. The bull dropped dead. In a few moments Kari was out of sight.

For a fortnight no one heard anything of him. I expected him to return to me, but he never came back. Even to this day no one knows what happened to him. Evidently those miserable engineers had driven him out of his mind. In his madness he must have gone back to the jungle and by the time he recovered his senses was so lost in its depths that he could not come back. When his mind returns to him, an elephant can never remember the road that he took in his insanity, and if he runs very far into the jungle he may never come back because the Spirit of the jungle seizes him.

Kari's last impression of human beings must have been so terrible that when the Spirit of the jungle asserted itself in him, he allowed it to lure him away forever from the habitations of men.

That is how it came about that I lost my friend and brother, the elephant. Though as an animal Kari is lost to me, my soul belongs to his soul and we shall never forget each other.